Teaching

on the

Inside

Book II

Surviving and Thriving in Correctional Education

by Pauline Geraci

Greystone
Educational Materials

All inquiries should be addressed to:
Greystone Educational Materials
P.O. Box 86
Scandia, MN 55073

ISBN: 978-1-881639-94-7

TABLE OF CONTENTS

DEDICATION

I would like to dedicate this book to my father who inspired me to write through his own writing and interesting stories. I want to thank my mother for her creative spirit and innovative teaching. I would also like to thank my husband for editing and keeping me focused on writing and finishing my book.

INTRODUCTION

Understand your purpose in life by feeling your heart's desires.
~ Marcia Wieder

This book is not theoretical. It is a collection of practical ideas and techniques which you can use immediately to rejuvenate you, your relationships at work, and make your teaching more effective and more enjoyable for you and your students. Readers will benefit most from this book if they are willing to be reflective about their own practice and explore new ways in which to grow personally and professionally.

This book is not only for the seasoned correctional educator but the new one as well. New educators can experience burn out and lack of motivation just as easily as seasoned correctional educators.

Most of us teaching in a correctional setting did not plan on teaching in prison. We were not told that teaching in a prison was an option. Before becoming correctional educators, some of us were elementary teachers, nurses, former nuns, or former military. Many of us just fell into our profession. Now that we are here, what do we do about it?

Correctional education isn't viewed as a field or specialty. Correctional educators are often seen as blessed souls doing the Lord's work. Even our students question us as to why we are teaching in prison. I will get questions like, "Why are you teaching us when you can be in a real school?" So, as a new teacher you find yourself in a strange paramilitary setting. It is like living in another country. You have to learn to negotiate and navigate a different culture, learn a new language, and try and understand different mores and norms. You also have to juggle the dual role of compassionate humanitarian with the demands of security. You basically have to recreate your teaching strategies and often cope with less than ideal settings and students.

Once you settle in and have been around for a while there are still things to cope with. If you were that young and motivated teacher, you may now be experiencing burn out. You may not enjoy what you do anymore. You have lost your passion and don't look forward to work, only your time off. In order to keep going as a correctional educator, you basically have to reinvent yourself.

Regardless of how long they have been teaching, few correctional educators are doing things as well as they possibly could. There are always opportunities for new ideas and attitudes.

The first thing is for you to be aware of what is going on with yourself and your teaching. You must not be afraid to look at yourself and your teaching with scrutiny. You have to be able to admit you may be like stale bread. In many households we often throw out stale bread. Stale bread should present an opportunity, not a problem. Stale bread doesn't have to be made into bread crumbs. Stale bread can be revived easily. Bread that is rock hard, though, may not be salvageable. Look at yourself carefully and from a fresh perspective. Are you too stale to save or do you need to move on and discover the work you are supposed to be doing?

The second thing is to be open to change. Change takes work, and it may not be easy. We not only need to change, but we need to transform ourselves. Don't get caught up in the same old scripts we act out every day. You have the power to write a whole new script for yourself. If you are willing to take the necessary steps toward changing yourself and your teaching, you will open yourself up to greater self-awareness, self-confidence and personal empowerment.

The third thing is for you to enjoy yourself and have fun. The late songwriter Warren Zevon was a guest on the David Letterman show. David asked a rather interesting question. The question was something like, "Knowing what you know now about your cancer, is there anything that you've learned or would try to do if you had it to do all over again?" Warren Zevon replied, "Yes, I'd try to enjoy every sandwich." Teaching in prison is hard enough without really enjoying what you are doing. If we keep looking forward to Friday then we aren't enjoying the moment and truly embracing what we do. I hope that this book will encourage correctional educators to try new things to develop yourself, your teaching and your students' learning. *Try and enjoy every sandwich.*

At the beginning of each chapter I have placed a checklist for you to contemplate before reading the chapter. Just consider this a little pre-reading stimulation. I suggest taking enough time to think about the questions, possibly by keeping a reading journal. At the end of the chapters there are activities for you to try.

In this book as in my first one, I have short vignettes at the beginning of each chapter about something that happened to a correctional educator. I don't put these in to scare new teachers. Rather I put them in for new and seasoned veterans so you can be reminded of where you work. Also these vignettes show the dichotomy of our jobs. We have to be caring individuals but balance it with security issues. We all get caught up in our day-to-day activities and lose sight of what is important. Every once in a while we need a reminder to keep us in focus and bring us back to the reality of where we work.

Chapter 1

BURNOUT

YOU AND I ARE THE ONLY ONES WHO WILL KNOW

An offender tutor went to get ice to melt for the fish tank because it was purified compared to the tap water in the prison. The teacher had him put the ice in a closet to melt. The offender kept asking her if he could check the ice. She knew that it would not be melted yet and wondered why he kept asking her. During lunch she went and looked at the ice buckets. Some melting had occurred and she saw why the offender had been so insistent about asking if he could look at the ice. In one of the buckets were several pounds of hamburger meat and an onion stolen from the kitchen. She confronted the offender later that afternoon. He admitted taking it and placing it in the buckets. She told him that she would have to report him and was very disappointed that he took advantage of her in his position of tutor. He asked her not to report him because they were the only two who knew what had occurred and he wouldn't say anything.

What happened and what would you do?   (See end of chapter.)

BURNOUT

Before you read this section think about the following statements.
Mark each statement:

A for agree
D for disagree
? if you are undecided

1. I still have the flame for teaching in corrections.	
2. My flame is slowly burning out.	
3. My flame is gone. I feel like a dead battery.	
4. I feel it is possible to rekindle that flame for teaching again.	
5. I just go to work and do the least possible to survive and then go home.	
6. My attitude is poor.	
7. My morale is low.	
8. I find joy in my work.	
9. I am passionate about my profession.	
10. My job is just a way to make ends meet.	
11. I have given up hoping that joy is something I might expect from work.	
12. It is unrealistic to expect my work to mean more than just the next paycheck.	
13. I enjoy life's challenges, and I learn from everything that happens in my life.	
14. I live each day with passion and power.	
15. I have feelings of emotional exhaustion and fatigue.	

16. I have negative attitudes toward my students.	
17. I have a loss of feelings of accomplishment on the job.	
18. I feel drained and used up.	
19. I have feelings of dread at the thought of having to put in another day on the job.	
20. I put distance between myself and others.	
21. I have developed a detached concern.	
22. I have become cynical and feel calloused toward others in the organization.	
23. There is a lack of feedback in my job.	
24. I feel lack of control or autonomy in my job.	
25. I am absent from my job a lot.	
26. I exert very little effort on the job.	
27. My quality of life has diminished.	

Nothing is really work unless you would rather be doing something else. ~ *James Matthew Barrie*

If you are bored with your work or have ever secretly hoped that something will happen at your place of work so that your class will be cancelled, your attitude needs an upgrade or you may be suffering from burnout. Do you tell people you work in a prison or do you tell them your job is a prison? You may be suffering from burnout. Symptoms of burnout are easy to identify and include physical exhaustion, detachment, negative attitudes toward your students, and a loss of feelings of accomplishment on the job. Through your behavior, you are expressing job dissatisfaction and that you don't care anymore.

One educator who was experiencing job dissatisfaction noted, "I've been in trouble for everything for the past six months with the state. I've just been trying to provide the best programming. I've learned not to try anything, do as I'm told, no matter how stupid the idea is or how it doesn't make sense, then things will go smoothly." Another educator commented, "Don't buck the system and you'll be okay!" This comment we have all heard many times, "The state doesn't care about us, we are as much a number as the inmates."

In a 2009 Washington State Workplace Confidence Survey, 75% of those surveyed said they would like to do something they love and 40% responded that if there no barriers like time or money, they would change careers.

If you think nobody cares if you're alive, try missing a car payment. ~ *Flip Wilson*

It is more than likely that every correctional educator at one time or another will experience personal or professional burnout. You've seen these teachers and maybe you have been one of them. They come in to work at the last minute. They don't care whether students sit at their desks bored out of their minds. They sit at the desk and do not interact with the students. They do the same thing everyday. The teacher is bored and their students are bored. They are the ones who say that their students can't learn anything. They are the ones who say I have given up on the students who don't want to do anything. The teacher tells you that some of these students can just sit at their desks all day, and as long as they are quiet, they could care less. They only have enough energy for the students who show some interest. You probably have heard this comment before, "This is the easiest job in the world. All I have to do is show up on time. I can sit in my class and do nothing day after day, but as long as I just show up no one cares. I love this job." Or, "I'm only here for the paycheck and I leave at 4:00 PM, regardless."

The above teachers are susceptible to developing emotional exhaustion and fatigue if they haven't already. These people are experiencing job burnout.

We as correctional educators are faced with the challenge of creating an atmosphere, environment, circumstances and lessons that will allow our students to succeed. The realities of our classroom life have made teaching in corrections a stressful occupation. But what do we do for ourselves? What kind of atmosphere and environment do we create for ourselves?

Do you know that in 2006 the average American spent 1,804 hours a year at work? Why would you spend over 1,804 hours doing something you don't find satisfying? Given the amount of time we spend at work, just imagine what our lives would be like if we made a change in the way we experience work.

One thing we can do is to stop blaming ourselves for how we feel. Studies by Maslach and Jackson indicate that the primary sources of burnout are related to organizational conditions and personal characteristics. Organizational conditions are factors that are unique to where we work. Personal characteristics are those that are unique to each of us like our age or sex. The biggest contributors to job stress are role conflict and role ambiguity. We all come from so many backgrounds and then we are thrown in to a completely different culture. We have to be security minded but we also have to be caring and nurturing individuals. We are constantly in conflict with our true selves and what is expected of us.

Many correctional educators lack a definition of who they are, what their mission is and how they fit in as professionals in a correctional setting. Teaching is a people profession; our mission would be rather meaningless without our students. Teaching in a correctional setting becomes an exercise in understanding oneself in relationship to where and who we are. These ubiquitous issues in the process of understanding ourselves are personal and in need of close examination by all correctional educators. One of my challenges as a correctional educator for the past 16 years has been the questioning and redefining of my identity. I have had to teach while feeling a sense of imbalance and discomfort, but the introspection has been well worth it. Here is something to think about: Is what you do a calling or a job? Does it resonate with who you are?

Are you as motivated now as when you first started teaching in corrections? Do you feel good about your attitude and your morale? Is your morale at an all-time high or all-time low? Does your day turn you or do you turn the day? Do you find yourself saying, "Thank goodness it's Friday?" Do you find yourself saying, "I'm just doing my job" rather than "I'm going to create my job?" Do you just count your years in service or do you make your years in service count? If you answered yes to the above questions, then now is the time to revive your morale and rededicate yourself to your profession. Now is the time to recharge your batteries, your attitude toward yourself and your profession. Now is the time to meditate on your life and how you can make it better. Discover what matters most to you and make your life into a true reflection of your ideas, beliefs and attitudes.

I'm reminded of a Ziggy cartoon when thinking of burn out. Ziggy is talking to his bird Josh saying that he thinks he is in a rut. The only relief he gets from his daily routines are from his weekly routines. Ziggy tells Josh that starting tomorrow he is going to do something about it. Josh then comments, "That would be very inspiring if he didn't give that same speech at least once a week."

How can you avoid burnout or make a comeback from the position of hating or being overwhelmed by your profession?

The first thing you need to do is "Be there." Where are you today at work? Are you actually there in mind and spirit? Are you totally focused? If we decide to not be "there" then we need to get out.

Next you need to work from the inside out. In other words, you need to start with yourself before you can make changes on the outside. Ask yourself: "Can I afford not to change?" You will never realize your greatest potential if you have lost your energy, enthusiasm, and passion.

Ships are safe in harbor, but that is not what ships are built for.
~ *Anonymous*

If you don't like change, you're going to like irrelevance a lot less.
~ *Tom Feltenstein*

The challenge for correctional educators is to keep playing the same music that made you want to teach in prison in the first place while keeping your teaching fresh, new, original, stimulating, and effective. You need to continually grow professionally and individually so you will have a chance to provide the best possible service to your students.

Teaching in a prison is emotionally and physically draining. Even though most educators love what they do and are passionate about their profession, teaching in prison can take its toll. Correctional educators need to take care of themselves and balance their professional life with their personal life, or they run a high potential for experiencing job dissatisfaction. You need to adopt positive coping mechanisms that help ward off burnout. This includes maintaining balance by keeping your teaching fresh through continued learning and personal growth, increased activity in your profession, and reestablished contact with friends and family. Develop networks of professional and personal support. Let others know when you are experiencing stress. You can't do all of this alone.

Why do you teach? You need to reevaluate why you teach. Are you in it for the money or are you doing something you love? Does teaching allow you to perform to your highest potential? Do you feel valued and appreciated? Do you play to your strengths and gifts? If the joy of teaching is gone, identify where the misery is coming from. First let's look at why your students come to school.

Why do your students want to attend school? In an article written by Raphael Schlesinger in the *Journal of Correctional Education*, the following were some reasons given by offenders for attending school:

- To congregate with friends and associates.
- Pose as learners because that is how to manipulate the correctional system. Make it like you are doing something if you aren't doing anything.
- Get out of the cell.
- Get some fresh air on the walk to and from the school building.
- Get paid.
- Exchange contraband.
- Sell.
- Avoid a kitchen assignment.
- Gamble.
- An alternative to being bored in the cell.
- Don't get along with a cellie.
- Killing time.
- Doing the little old hustle.
- Develop skills.
- Get a GED.
- Participating in school makes them feel good and increases self-esteem.
- Want to learn for their children.
- Do something positive and practical.
- It is the only good thing about being in prison.
- Do it for their family.

Why do you still show up at your job? Do you still love your job?

What attracted you to teaching in prison in the first place? What are some aspects of teaching that make you want to keep teaching? Does it allow you to explore your personal limits? Does it allow you to make a difference in individual lives? Is it exciting, well paid, demanding and challenging? Do you believe that what you do is special and valued? Do you believe that all of your students have a chance at being successful? Is it your students?

Do you remember the special moments with your students? I remember a most recent moment. I was conducting a Reading Is Fundamental Book Fair in the visiting room of the correctional facility where I work. It was family night. Children were there to choose free books to take home with them. There wasn't a huge turnout so I wasn't thrilled. Once the children chose their books there was a transformation in that room. As I went around the room observing, I saw a little girl on a mat laying down and reading from her new book. I saw an offender father with his child on his lap, the mother nearby, reading to his child from the new book. I saw families reading together. I saw the offenders in another light and it was heartwarming. Later that evening a father came up with his children and with tears in his eyes he thanked me for making the book fair happen.

I am sure that many of us have had something similar occur in their career. An offender student comes up to me and tells me he was so ashamed that he couldn't spell. He said, "When I get letters from my mother or wife I won't answer them because I don't want them to know that I can't spell well. My wife has a college degree, and it is embarrassing." Wow, what an opportunity to make a difference in someone's life!

Another offender who played high school football took a test and scored quite high. Later he came up to my desk to tell me that was the highest he had ever scored in anything educational. In high school they only made him play ball and not concentrate on his academics.

I asked one of my ESL students how he learned math if he didn't attend school. He commented, "I learned math and writing working in the pot fields with my family. A teacher working along side us to make more money taught me my math and writing right there in the fields."

I commented on an ESL student's use of the English language. I asked him where he learned his English. He proceeded to enlighten me, "When I came here from Mexico the first six months I only ate cheeseburgers. Anytime someone asked us what we wanted to eat while at work, I said cheeseburger because that was the only word I knew how to say in English. I finally got tired of eating cheeseburgers so I started learning English."

There are funny moments as well. One student asked me what was wrong and I replied, "Stuff." He asked me, "What stuff?" I answered, "Just stuff." The offender retorted, "The last time I told a cop 'stuff,' I got arrested."

There are also many sad but profound moments. I hosted a poetry group where the offenders would attend workshops and write poetry.

An offender in the workshop commented during a workshop on manhood, "I would be locked in my room at 14 by my parents. I mean with a padlock. I would be crying and daydreaming about having a child to love and that I could be a good father too." The poetry workshop gave this offender a chance to really express his emotions, hurts, and feelings.

Another offender in the poetry group, a victim of torture and a survivor of the Khmer Rouge genocide in Cambodia, came to the group with the idea that he could not write poetry. He was very shy and hardly spoke. Today, this same man is one of the most prolific poets in the group and is not afraid to speak up about his work. "Poetry gave me a way to write away some painful experiences. It's hard to write those experiences. I have to feel the emotions again. But when I get it onto paper, I feel like, wow, I'm happy." This same man recently published a book of poems through a grant in Minnesota.

I remember a very special moment after a Spoken Word session in which the poetry group performed for the rest of the education department. "The men performed with closed eyes and clenched fists. The men spoke of their lives, their anger, and their sadness. It was totally transformative. You could see eyes light up and high-voltage smiles emanating from their faces."

During a Theater of the Oppressed workshop I heard the following comments from the men, "It's like we're kids again." "When we come in here we can forget for a couple of hours where we are. We can relax and have fun without it being all 'mean mugs'." "We can laugh in here. You don't get much real laughter in prison."

During a book making session, a group of men sat at tables wearing colorful strips of ribbon around their necks, gluing, cutting, and sewing. It looked like a ladies sewing circle. They talked about picnics with their children and how much their children were going to love the books.

One student made a book for his mother since he had no children. He said his mother had not called or written him since his incarceration. "I wrote the book so maybe she would finally talk to me. It worked because she wrote me to say that the book I made was wonderful and she was so proud of what I did."

I could go on and on as all of you could. There are so many precious moments that occur in our teaching careers. These moments all keep me going and keep me from burning out. I want to influence the life of someone. I want to make a positive difference.

To learn and never be filled, is wisdom; to teach and never be weary, is love. ~ Author Unknown

Activity:

Now it's your turn. Write down the reasons why you teach in prison.

Activity:

Create a Philosophy of Teaching Statement. A Philosophy of Teaching Statement is a brief reflective essay concerning one's understanding about how students learn, how instruction can best assist that learning, and actions that you take to enact such instruction. It may also include your teaching goals, your learning goals for students, and areas in which you would like to further improve your teaching abilities. Your philosophy of teaching statement should reflect your personal values and the needs of your students. It should be no more than one page in length.

Do you maintain a personal life that is separate from work?

Don't give up a balanced lifestyle for one that only revolves around your students and teaching. Leave work at work and enjoy your life at home. I know, sometimes I will see things during my days off that I can use in the classroom. My mind is constantly going and I continually have ideas pop into my head. I have to stop the thoughts and tell myself to let it go. In the scheme of things, it isn't important to come up with ideas at this moment. I don't take papers home to grade or read. I just want to enjoy my time off and enjoy my family.

One minute is all you need.

I want you to think about what I am going to say here. Most of our offender students are incarcerated because it only took one minute to make the wrong decision or to do the wrong thing. That one minute changed the rest of their life. In one minute you can change your attitude and in that one minute change your entire day. You may not be able to change your whole life in this one minute. A bad attitude can create absolute misery. We may feel that our attitude is justified, but it still makes us miserable. Maintaining a healthy attitude not only can change each and every day, but it:

- protects your health
- may extend your life
- increases your enjoyment of life
- helps you deal with stress
- increases our success at work
- improves our relationships

Activity:

Think like you want to be. Believe you can change and be the person you want to be. If you want to be happy and less stressed, think that way. Smile more and stress less. Don't let your thoughts control you, control your thoughts. Remember, it takes about 28 days with continuous, consistent and positive re-enforcement, to break a habit. So work on thinking like you want to be each and every day and don't give up.

Activity:

Don't set limits for yourself. Do you live thinking that any situation is an opportunity for success or do you believe that sooner or later something bad is going to happen? Try looking at all situations as opportunities for success. Think about those training sessions that bore you to tears. You've been there, you've done that. Now go into that next training session with an open mind and see what you can glean from it. So it may not be useful at work, maybe you can use what they covered at the conference in your personal life. Maybe you can help someone else with what you learned at the conference. Even if you just got one thing from the conference that one thing may be enough to motivate you or challenge you.

Find a purpose and your passion will follow. ~ Mac Anderson

Where would you work for free?

I'm sure we all have heard the buzzword, "sustainability." It is used when referring to the environment. How can we sustain the earth and be good stewards of the environment. But sustainability should also be about people. We need to ask how we can sustain ourselves and our fellow teachers so we can continue doing what we enjoy.

One answer is our perspective on what we do and whether we consider what we do valuable. The following comments came from a retired public school teacher who volunteered at a jail: "I am an 85 year old retired public school teacher. I have been teaching in jail for the past 12 years. The time I spend at the Washington County Jail is about 6-8 hours a week. It is the most valuable and treasured time of my life. I am giving something away and expect nothing back. I may be the first person in an inmate's life who never expected anything from him or her and still devoted a piece of my life to them. When I burn out from this job, it will be from arthritis and the inability to push a cart of books down a long cement walk. Reading, writing, and arithmetic is just as much fun for me today as when my third grade teacher got stressed because I finished my assignment before she reached her desk" *Dorothy Haas*

The world is divided into two types of people; those who are happy, healthy, pleasant and cheerful, and those who are unhappy, unpleasant and sad. The difference is people in the first group evaluate themselves and try to improve, while the second group evaluates others and blames.
~ Dr. William Glaser

Go back and reread the checklist at the beginning of the chapter. Have your thoughts changed?

YOU AND I ARE THE ONLY ONES WHO WILL KNOW

What actually happened?

When the tutor asked her not to write him up because they would be the only ones that would know, the teacher told him that she was writing him up anyways. He was supposed to set an example and he was being sneaky. He basically lied. She called a correctional officer to pick-up the evidence and for them to take the offender out of her classroom.

What should she have done?

Exactly what the teacher did. She also quit letting the tutors go get ice to melt for fish water. If you constantly have to check up on what your tutors or students are up to then they shouldn't be doing it anymore.

Chapter 2

COMPLACENCY

THE MOTHER'S DAY CARD

The teacher was given a Mother's Day card during class from an offender. She never felt comfortable around the offender. In the card, the offender mentioned things about an affair with her, that he liked her smile, and thought she was beautiful. He told her that he was getting out in three years and wanted to be her friend. He said he had two former teachers on his visiting list now.

What happened and what would you do? (See end of chapter.)

COMPLACENCY

Before you read this section think about the following statements.
Mark each statement:

A for agree
D for disagree
? if you are undecided

1. I have been teaching in corrections for so long that I know all there is to know.	
2. I don't need to learn anymore about being a correctional educator.	
3. I don't have much enthusiasm about my job anymore.	
4. I don't pay attention to details.	
5. Sometimes I feel too comfortable in my job.	
6. I am not happy with my supervisor or the organization.	
7. I stand up for the offender when the offender is blamed.	
8. I find myself relying too much on offenders to help me.	
9. I have felt uncomfortable with something inappropriate an offender said but let it go.	
10. It doesn't matter if I write up an offender because corrections staff will do nothing about it.	
11. I don't care how I dress. Jeans and sandals are always acceptable.	
12. I don't treat every incident, real or practice, as an actual incident until proven otherwise.	
13. I forget to wear my ID badge or card at work.	
14. On occasion, I've come to work, run-down or not totally alert.	
15. I don't look to see if there are weaknesses in my daily routine.	

16. I misinterpret situations.	
17. I fail to predict or anticipate changing conditions.	
18. I have memory lapses.	
19. I forget to lock things, turn off the lights, etc…	
20. I don't pay attention.	
21. I get distracted easily.	
22. I experience task overload.	
23. I experience cognitive overload.	
24. I feel excess stress or fatigue.	
25. I feel I have not had adequate training or preparation.	
26. My motivation feels low.	
27. I have a pattern of overconfidence.	
28. I experience anger and job frustration.	
29. I lack the confidence to perform my job.	
30. I misjudge actual risks in situations.	
31. I exceed my personal limits	
32. I don't listen to advice.	
33. I take unnecessary risks.	

If we sit by and become complacent and put our heads in the sand, we're complicit. ~ Shelley Morrison

They'd taken shortcuts. They'd taken risks. They'd developed an "It won't happen to me" attitude. What could go wrong? If you are not thinking about what could go wrong every day, all day, while at work, you are not going to be completely safe. I am not talking about becoming paranoid and obsessed with this thinking, but it must be in the back of your mind. Remember, the time that you are at greatest risk is when you least expect something bad is about to happen or everything is going great in your life. You have a smile on your face and a spring in your step. This is exactly when you need to think ahead and consider:

Who are you working with?
What will they be doing?
What could go wrong?

Complacency is defined as the feeling you have when you are satisfied with yourself, especially when accompanied by unawareness of actual dangers or deficiencies.

Another term for complacency is "Satisficing." This term, coined by Herb Simon, means "To accept a choice or judgment as one that is good enough, one that satisfies." When we satisfice, we accept a satisfactory outcome and stop looking further once we are satisfied. For instance, when I was looking for a mountain bike with my husband, I saw one that was a cool looking burnt orange color with neat designs on it. It also seemed to be a good price. I wanted it. My husband on the other hand wanted to look at the bikes further online so he could find the best overall deal for his money. He told me I was "satisficing." In other words, we may look for an answer to a problem and end up with a mediocre one, but with a bit more time and effort, we could get a better answer. Satisficing does us a disservice because it imposes limits on what we can achieve.

Complacency is an attitude that determines how we respond to given situations. If you ask someone what complacency is, they would be hard pressed to give you a definition. If you asked what it looked like, they may be able to describe it. Complacency is difficult to define but you know it when you see it, especially in others. According to Peter Braun, Performance Consultant for the National Institute of Corrections, Peninsula College, "Complacency is about assumptions. It is based on mental images rather than what is in front of you. It is based on memories rather than facts." One teacher described complacency as, "An idiot who believes he or she knows all the answers." Another teacher said, "Complacency looks like a person on automatic pilot, detached emotionally, aimless and unmotivated. Complacency can set it in once passion for your vocation has waned."

Complacency: The Victory Disease

In the book, <u>Getting it right: American Military Reforms after Vietnam to the Gulf War and Beyond</u>, Victory Disease, by definition, "brings defeat to previously victorious nations or military due to three basic symptoms: arrogance, complacency, and the habit of using established patterns to solve military problems." Even though complacency is listed as a symptom of the disease, I like to think that the Victory Disease is in itself complacency.

So what are the some of the symptoms of complacency?

Accepting Lower Standards of Performance. What are your standards of performance? Are they the same as they were when you first started teaching? Do you have high standards of performance for yourself, your co-workers, and your students?

Lack of Desire and Commitment for Excellence. Do you make an effort to keep abreast of what is going on in corrections and correctional education? Do you read the Journal of Correctional Education? Do you read up on current trends in corrections? You don't just start working in corrections education and think you have reached the pinnacle of your profession. There is always something to learn.

Boredom and Inattention. Work has become monotonous to you. Day in and day out it is the same thing over and over again. You can't wait to go home.

Satisfied with the Status Quo. You accept things the way they are. You don't want to upset the apple cart. You like your little routine and don't want things changed. You are in your happy place and you don't want to mess that up by doing anything different.

Ask people at work, "If you are not complacent, please stand up?" I bet everyone will jump to his or her feet. What is strange about complacency is that no one admits to being complacent because no one ever believes they are. It is kind of like having bad breath. Many times we don't know our breath smells like garlic until someone brings it to our attention. Then we cup our hand around our mouth, exhale a puff of air, and sure enough our breath could gag a maggot. It sure is easy to identify complacency in others but not in ourselves.

If you research articles on complacency you will find dozens citing how complacency kills, injures, and maims. Complacency is always blamed for safety and security problems.

Complacency on the job injures and kills. According to Linda Werfelman, *AeroSafety World,* "72 percent of aircraft accidents in the United States are caused by unsafe acts, not unsafe conditions." There was either a deliberate breach of the rules or routine, or small-scale violations.

No one gets up in the morning saying I am going to let my guard down because nothing will happen to me. Complacency can spread like the flu from one worker to another. One employee sees a co-worker taking a shortcut and figures, "If he can do it, why can't I?" You can't afford to let complacency take over in your workplace.

In New York State the Department of Correctional Services, Commissioner Glenn S. Goord, put out a press release: "*Staff complacency contributed to escape from Elmira prison.*" He states, "It resulted from complacency manifested in a widespread breakdown in Departmental practices, long-time policies and security procedures. The inmates recognized and took advantage of these lapses. Staff complacency allowed the inmates to identify, smuggle and utilize contraband and other material to enable their escape."

In another state, Arizona, complacency was the key in the 15-day Arizona takeover. "The incident at the Morey Unit evolved out of a rich combination of complacency, inexperience, lack of professionalism, and a lack of situational awareness."

According to police officer, Patrick Fagan, "*Complacency is the*

28

police officers number one enemy. Police complacency is non-recognition of danger and a false security of contentment. This condition is a rarity among recruits who have recently graduated from a law enforcement academy. The new cadets are more cautious and more wary." This statement is contrary to the myth that prisons and jails get so many new unprepared employees, that more than likely misconduct will occur. In research by Susan W. McCampbell and Elizabeth P. Layman, *Investigating Allegations of Staff Sexual Misconduct with Inmates: Myths and Realities*, "While some rookie officers have been involved with misconduct, a disturbing observation is that many officers involved in sexual misconduct are those with many years on the job and who hold rank in the organization."

It is a natural human response to ease up when things are going great. Look at marriages. Before people get married they work hard at appearances, how they act, and how they come across to the other person. Then when they do get married they are not the same people. This also occurs with diet and exercise. I train people who want to fit into their wedding dress and look great when they walk down the aisle. Once the wedding is over, no more gym sessions. They let themselves go and don't even see it until it is too late and then they want me to help them lose weight again. Heck I've been there as well. I started gaining weight and just didn't see how much weight I was gaining until I went shopping and tried on a pair of pants. The size I tried on certainly wasn't the size I used to wear. That sure woke me up. How can we not see what we are doing to ourselves when we look in the mirror every day? When we finally do see it we take action. When things don't go well we work harder. We have a zone of comfort we fall into, and complacency is what we sometimes need to bring us back to reality.

As you can see from the above incidents complacency does damage. But what does it look like? How do we know someone is complacent? How do we know we are complacent?

The longer we stay on the job, the more we grow comfortable dealing with offenders, and complacency may set in. Complacency brings a relaxation of our own personal safety practices. Through familiarity, we may lower our attention to detail and stop looking for signs of potential threat. We may think, "It isn't going to happen to me. It's the other person."

29

Complacency is a comfortable state of mind oblivious to any danger that is around us. We regularly experience complacency in our personal lives and at our jobs. The key is awareness. The places we feel the most familiar or comfortable in, like our classrooms, can be the most dangerous. When we feel overly comfortable and confident, we often forget things are subject to change and can become unsafe in an instant.

Did you know that a positive mood is likely to trigger less careful thinking strategies? According to the authors of "Mood Effects on Eyewitness Memory: Affective Influences on Susceptibility to Misinformation," in the *Journal of Experimental Social Psychology*, "When we are feeling really good, the whole world looks good. We aren't as vigilant. We don't notice things are out of sorts. We basically look at things through so-called 'rose-colored glasses.' Good moods signal a nonthreatening environment." I am not saying we should be negative and in a lousy mood all the time. We should look at security in a more systematic, more attentive way as if everything is not okay. We must learn to be more aware of our surroundings and be alert to the possibility of danger. To be safe, you must expect the worst to happen. Life is what happens when you least expect it. You do not need to be paranoid; you just need to be vigilant, even when there is nothing apparently going on.

A problem that occurs with complacency is that most co-workers don't call you on it. We see it in others but fail to see it in ourselves; and then it is too late. Think about it: Has anyone told you that they are concerned with your behavior? There is an old Yiddish saying, "If one person calls you a jackass, ignore him. If a second person calls you a jackass, think about it. If a third person calls you a jackass, get a saddle."

How many times have teachers gotten into trouble without any previous red flags raised by the staff. The teacher may have never admitted to anything; she just resigned. The rest of the staff is in disbelief, asking, "What did we miss? What didn't we see? Why didn't we catch this? Maybe we could have helped her. She did a good job otherwise." We have to take care of each other. We can't look at the task of telling another co-worker that something is wrong like nailing Jell-O to the wall. We can't worry about what the other person will think about us. We have to do more confronting when we see unacceptable behavior or behavior that can be a precursor to trouble. I certainly hope that we would appreciate the same feedback from others.

Sometimes it's the people we're working with and sometimes it's the situation. When people we work with stop challenging one another, then we eventually become too comfortable, causing boredom and eventual complacency.

Staff boredom is not necessarily bad as far as the offenders are concerned. According to some offenders, "the bored ones hate their jobs but they make the offenders lives harder. The bored ones go around looking for something to do. They look for people to write up and they perform a lot of cell searches to keep busy."

If you have something to say, speak up. Don't just watch from the sidelines as others head down the wrong path. Is it that much easier to not get involved then to say something to prevent a problem from happening?

Another problem we encounter with complacency is in allowing others to define our worth. Because we allow others to change our boundaries we are uncertain what they look like anymore. Offenders sense they can challenge you just for the sake of getting their way. You make it easy for offenders to bully you. You need to be clear with your boundaries. What is nonnegotiable to you? What are you unwilling to change? Are they healthy boundaries? What do they look like for you?

When we are complacent, we prefer comfort to chaos. You've seen what happens when your peers challenge things. You find it easier to let others get in trouble while you don't draw attention to yourself and continue to collect your paycheck. According to the offenders, the paycheck collectors are lazy. They don't want others, including offenders to bother them. Offenders call these paycheck collectors, "active assholes." They basically tell others don't ask me anything, leave me alone. Offenders stay clear of these people because they know they aren't going to get away with small talk and can't ask for anything. Your co-workers will stay away from you as well because you put up a wall around yourself. You don't let others in and you won't say anything because you don't want to "stir the pot."

Many times we don't say anything because we don't want to upset anyone because it makes them uncomfortable. Make people feel uncomfortable! Tell it like it is when you see it. You may make people feel uncomfortable but maybe you can prevent someone from losing their job. I have read many incidents where a correctional educator or corrections staff lost their job here in the United States and overseas, but no one called attention to their behavior until they got in trouble.

When you become complacent you expect less from yourself and others no longer expect much from you. Offenders can sense your complacency. They will be constantly sizing you up. They will observe your demeanor, presence, physical fitness, commitment, and experience. As one offender put it, "It's like going into a bar. The girl gives you a wink, and it's on." Raise the bar for yourself and expect more of yourself.

Professionalism is the key according to Susan W. McCampbell and Elizabeth P. Layman. "Initial breaches of professional boundaries may have been seemingly minor issues that appear to have little or no consequence. But small breaches of professionalism compound over time."

The way you present yourself is how offenders will perceive you and treat you. Dress as a professional. Wear jeans sparingly. Iron your clothes, clean your shoes. Dress with care. Speak as you would in any professional setting. Do not become familiar or too comfortable with your students. It is human nature to want to become close to the people with whom we work. This should be true, only to a point, as a correctional educator. Personal information about oneself such as your address, phone numbers, and pictures of your family should never be shared with students. When you share information, according to offenders, "You have a personal confidence with the offender and open the door for further manipulation." The manipulation is a surprisingly subtle, slow, insidious process, as quiet as an inmate asking staff to check on mail or giving an inmate too much paper because they ask for it.

In the book, <u>Games Criminals Play</u>, there is a chapter called "Downing a Duck," which describes gaining personal confidence in great detail. A duck is an institution employee who can be manipulated. An offender will develop a duck by watching and getting to know a person. They watch to see how you act and dress. They get to know what you like and dislike. They also get the duck to be on a first name basis. They watch to see if you will break minor rule violations.

Here is a recent example of "downing a duck." A former prison secretary was sentenced to six months in federal prison for having sex with an inmate she was supposed to be supervising. The individual was a 14-year Bureau of Prisons veteran. She said she and the inmate, who was assigned to clean her office, began to have conversations and realized they had similar interests. She also obtained a cell phone with a non-local phone number so the offender could call her without raising suspicion and admitted she gave him contraband that included photographs with explicit sexual poses.

In one school district in Texas that oversees the corrections education program, within one year, there were twelve employees who lost their jobs because they were compromised. Five of these employees were going through a divorce or a death in their family. The oldest was 53 years of age and the youngest was 24. One was a 16-year veteran and another had only been working for 3 months. As you can see, compromise can happen to anyone.

I asked a few offenders about how they go about setting up someone. One said, "You manipulate them. It is all in how friendly you can get with them. If they tell you about their outside life, where they live, what they do in their free time, actual places they go, that is when you know you got them." Another offender commented that they "look for new employees who are feeling isolated and a little inept." They try to become the employee's support group; happy to sympathize and say they'll protect them if trouble breaks out. Another told me, "I see this in teachers a lot. If you constantly tell your students you are going to do something to someone, then you should do it. If you don't take action, they are going to run all over you." Another offender said, "Look for someone who isn't sloppy, who follows the rules. It's a game with us. These are the ones that no one else would suspect. We ask them if they want to make a lot of money and if they fall for it then we got them. There are a lot of correctional workers who want the money. When they bring in pot or other things, the rest of the staff won't look twice at the ones who follow the rules. No one would suspect them." According to a March 2000 *Correctional Compass* article, "Inmates will concentrate on the soft and hard employees. Soft because of the inability or hesitancy to say no, combined with their understanding and sympathetic traits. Hard because inmates may feel that the hardness and the "by the book, no exceptions attitude" disguises a weakness in that individual."

No matter how long we have been working in a prison setting, we have to keep going back to the questions, "Where am I working? Who am I working with?" Think of the GED essay. When writing the essay, one has to keep going back to the main topic we are writing about. Many of our students don't focus on the topic and get off track. I also like to think of dealing with complacency as a view of Mt. Rainier or Mt. Fuji in Japan. If you have ever lived in Washington State or visited it, Mt. Rainer can be seen from 100 miles away. It all depends on where your view is. When you are driving on higher elevation you will see it clearly, but when the road dips or takes a turn you lose sight of the majestic mountain. Complacency is no different. Once we lose sight of where we are, we are going to get sidetracked and miss what we are supposed to be focusing on. If we don't keep focusing on where we work, we will get off track and get in trouble. Remind yourself, "I work in a prison."

Bottom line: Fly the jet, use the checklist, watch your buddy, communicate problems early, and debrief your lessons so others don't have to make the same mistakes. ~ Tony Kern

Activity:
What can you do to prevent complacency in the workplace? Have you thought about making a checklist for yourself? What things do you need to do before leaving the classroom? What do you need to do before you leave your desk and computer? How can you prevent complacency in your personal life? Do you have a checklist for leaving your car parked? Do you know where you are going to place valuables? Do you know where not to park? Do you always remember to lock your doors and roll up the windows?

Activity:
Mentally rehearse scenarios that may happen in the classroom.

What would you do in a medical emergency? What would you do if a fight broke out in your classroom? What would you do if someone attacked you? Conduct self-critiques, asking the question "what if" and focus on improving your training. How are you doing? Evaluate yourself. If you find that there is a need to change, make that change, not just for yourself, but also for your department and the organization as a whole.

Activity:

How can you prevent complacency in your professional life? Come up with a Professional Development Plan if you haven't already done so. Write down your goals for yourself as far as teaching. Ask yourself these questions:

- Do you want to further your education?
- Do you want to attend workshops or conferences?
- Where do you see yourself down the road?
- How are you going to get there?
- Where are you now professionally and personally?
- Where do you want to be professionally and personally?
- Visualize where you would like to be professionally.
- What does it look like?
- What does it feel like?
- Who are you with?
- What are you doing?
- Are you happy?

Go back and reread the checklist at the beginning of the chapter. Have your thoughts changed?

THE MOTHER'S DAY CARD

What did the teacher do?
She wrote up the offender.

The teacher should also:
1. Let the supervisor know what happened and give up the card.
2. Bring it out into the open.
3. Write up the offender for the inappropriate card.

It is ok to get cards from offenders in your classroom, as long as they are appropriate. You should thank the offender and then post it prominently in the classroom for all to see. You should also be wary of the same offender giving you more than one card. Just be aware and also pay attention to how you feel. Does it feel right? If not, then report it. If you feel uncomfortable then your instinct is telling you something. Listen to yourself.

Chapter 3

MINDLESSNESS VS. MINDFULNESS

YOU DON'T NEED TO DO IT ALL

The teacher taught GED/ABE classes. In addition he ran the in-house education television station, sponsored a book club and debate team. He also did a classroom newsletter and an Internet website for education. Besides this he brought in special guest speakers and wrote grants for class projects. He couldn't be everywhere, could he? Two of his offender tutors were allowed to have a camera to take pictures for the television station and for the Internet website. They went out to take pictures and then came back to download them to a thumb drive. They gave him the pictures but he never really had time to watch or look at everything they did. After all, he had so many other things to do.

What happened and what would you do? (See end of chapter.)

MINDLESSNESS VERSUS MINDFULNESS

Before you read this section think about the following statements.
Mark each statement:

> **A** for agree
> **D** for disagree
> **?** if you are undecided

1. I start my day on autopilot and sometimes don't know how I even got to work.	
2. When I deviate from my routine I sometimes forget to do things.	
3. I don't always pay attention to what I am doing.	
4. I am not as attentive or vigilant as I should be.	
5. I do things out of habit and repetition so I am not aware of what I am doing.	
6. I don't live in the present moment.	
7. I multi-task.	
8. I take on too many things at one time.	
9. Sometimes my mind is not at work.	
10. I feel too rushed.	
11. I try to slow down my thinking when I feel overwhelmed.	
12. I don't pay attention to what and how much I eat.	
13. I am open to new experiences.	
14. I am flexible and open-minded.	
15. I am always generating new ideas.	

16. I am curious.	
17. I can see things from many perspectives.	
18. I sometimes experience emotions that I am not conscious of until some time later.	
19. I tend to walk quickly to get where I am going without paying attention to what I experience along the way.	
20. I tend not to notice feelings of physical tension or discomfort until they really grab my attention.	
21. I forget a person's name almost as soon as I've been told it for the first time.	
22. It seems I am running on automatic without much awareness of what I'm doing.	
23. I rush through activities without being really attentive to them.	
24. I get so focused on the goal I want to achieve that I lose touch with what I am doing right now to get there.	
25. I do jobs or tasks automatically without being aware of what I am doing.	
26. I find myself listening to someone with one ear, doing something else at the same time.	
27. I am not what I think and feel.	
28. I can grasp and release my thoughts and emotions.	
29. I am aware of my thoughts and emotions.	
30. I am aware of my behavioral patterns.	
31. I believe I play a key role in creating and maintaining a great deal of my own tension and anxiety.	
32. My thoughts are constantly in the past or the future, not in the present.	
33. I don't react to things but mindfully choose an intentional response.	

No one imagines that a symphony is supposed to improve in quality as it goes along, or that the whole object of playing it is to reach the finale. The point of music is discovered in every moment of playing and listening to it. It is the same, I feel, with the greater part of our lives, and if we are unduly absorbed in improving them we may forget altogether to live them.
  ~ Alan Watts

What is mindlessness? According to Ellen Langer, professor in the Psychology Department at Harvard University, "It is the human tendency to operate on autopilot."

We lead much of our life on autopilot. For instance, is this your life: Wake-up, shower, eat, drive to work, work, and drive home, eat, watch TV, sleep, and repeat over again. Have you ever found yourself somewhere with no recollection of how you got there? You know it took several behaviors and decisions to get there, but you don't remember making the decisions and completing the sequence of tasks. We do this while driving every day. It's as if the vehicle drove itself. This is mindless behavior.

People sometimes move through daily regimes with little thought or alertness. The more routine and common the activity, the more likely a person will follow an unconscious routine to guide their actions. They will be completely unaware of what they are doing. For example, in the morning I always follow the same routine. I usually wash my teeth, floss and rinse; wash my face, put on makeup. It is usually a mindless activity. Not much thought goes into it because it is 4:30 in the morning and I don't want to engage my brain too much if at all possible. One morning I was running late so I did my routine out of order. In fact, it was so out of order, that when I got to work, horrors of all horrors, I had forgotten to put on my makeup. This is mindless activity, and social psychologists warn us that in this state we are particularly susceptible to marketing and social influence tactics. Now if I had actually been doing something that was dangerous, there would also have been a significant risk of injury in this mindless state.

In the past few years, hospitals have tried a new approach to decrease complications with patients. Eight hospitals reduced the number of deaths from surgery by more than 40% by using a checklist that helps doctors and nurses avoid errors, according to a report in *The New England Journal of Medicine*. They created checklists for surgeons, nurses, and staff. The checklists concentrated on activities that staff did daily, including routine surgeries. The checklists were similar to flight checklists for pilots. When the hospital staff adhered to these checklists, mortality in hospitals decreased by one half and complications decreased by one third. These simple checklists became a strategy to reduce morbidity and mortality.

How many injuries occur because people were just not thinking? How often do we get into a set work routine in which a sequence of behaviors is performed unconsciously? We take our mind off the process and put ourselves in automatic mode. This is fine if all these habitual behaviors are safe, but what if an event requires an immediate adjustment in our behavior, but our lack of awareness or mindlessness at the time prevents prompt reaction? Without even realizing it, our mindless work practice puts us at risk and everyone else near us. Mindlessness is most common when people are distracted, hurried, multitasking, and/or overloaded. For instance, when we are driving to work and see the other person in front of us talking on a cell phone, drinking a latte, and holding their cute, little, mini dog on their lap in front of the steering wheel. Meanwhile, yes, they are also trying to drive.

According to the Flight Safety Foundation, "More often than not, an individual cannot recall or verbalize the precise sequence of events leading up to the behavior or even remember components of the actual response itself such as – riding a bike, walking, driving a car, and even the mechanical acts of flying an airplane." These are all examples of mindless, highly over learned behaviors. We act on a mindless adherence to a set of operating procedures. In a fairly recent article in the *Journal of Consumer Research*, "If you are distracted by something like an incoming call on your cell phone, you are more apt to be susceptible to advertisements. You are likelier to buy based on subconscious, ad-influenced feelings when you are not focused." Why do you think they advertise on television so much?

We operate in a mindless state quite often. While sitting at home we watch television, cruise the Internet, and have a conversation with our loved ones. Sometimes we read a book and have the radio on or the television. We come home with the groceries and are greeted by our children or husband, put our keys down so we can put the groceries away and then when we need our car keys we can't find them. I admit it; I have been guilty of mindlessness. I was always trying to do several things at once. I am always trying to do as many things as possible. I try to pack in as much life as I can in a short amount of time. I just go and go and keep adding on more things to my schedule. I have had to stop, slow down, and focus. This is the practice of mindfulness. I am not always perfect when it comes to practicing mindfulness but at least I am trying. It has definitely made a difference in my personal and professional life.

Many times we think, so what? These mindless acts are inconsequential. Are they? We might be focused on our favorite television program when our spouse starts talking to us? Are we really listening? We may think so because we are nodding our head, maybe making a comment or two. But are we really focused on our spouse and what they are saying? This isn't inconsequential to your spouse. Your spouse may find it rude or that you are not interested in what he or she has to say. Will it really hurt you to actually mute the television and take the time to listen to your spouse or children? If you find your spouse is always reminding you to listen, then maybe you haven't really been listening.

When we misplace our keys, is that really a big deal? Misplacing our keys may cause us to be a little late getting to our destination. But when this mindlessness occurs at work, especially in a correctional setting, it isn't as inconsequential. We could break security procedures, cause a death, or lose our job.

Many times we follow the same mindless script day in and day out at work. We do things out of habit. A habit is mindless behavior. We don't think, we just react and do it. We come to work, get our keys, open our door, turn on the lights, turn on our computer, unlock things, and check our mail. We do this day in and day out. We take the path of least resistance by doing the same things over and over.

The Buddhist practice of mindfulness is the art of being in the present moment, or in other words being aware of the present moment, non-egoistic alertness, participatory observation, and awareness of change.

Mindfulness, as defined in Wikipedia, is "The practice whereby a person is intentionally aware of his or her thoughts and actions in the present moment, non-judgmentally. Mindfulness is applied to both bodily actions and the mind's own thoughts and feelings."

We are no longer happy as soon as we wish to be happier.
  ~ *Walter Savage Landor*

When people discuss mindfulness, they are referring to how mindfulness helps them enjoy the present moment, the now. We aren't thinking about what could have or should have been. We aren't thinking about how things will be in the future and not living here and now. Our minds and lives our like a helicopter on a never-ending hover pattern. Because we keep looking at the past and the future we don't know when to touch down and actually live our lives. Mindfulness may enhance our relationships because we will be more focused on what our loved ones are saying. We will be able to focus on who our loved ones really are and not what we want them to be. We will be able to appreciate and be fully engaged with the ones who are important in our lives. Mindfulness will make our meals more enjoyable. We will be able to taste the full flavor of each bite and fully savor the experience. We will be able to notice more on our walks through the neighborhood. Our perception will be enhanced. Mindfulness slows us down so we can truly experience all that life has to offer.

Dogs are great examples of living in the present moment. When my dog is riding in the car, that is all he is focused on, the experience. He sticks his nose out, sniffs the air for wonderful scents, the wind flaps his ears back and he has the ride of his life. He seems to experience sheer pleasure and joy. When I throw his tennis ball to him that is all he focuses on. He doesn't care about anything around him, just the ball. I've even taken him to dog parks to play ball with other dogs. He ignores the dogs and only wants the ball; he becomes one with the ball. When my dog wants to be petted, he sits down with me and demands petting. If he wants me to rub under his neck he lets me know by pushing his wet cold nose into my hand. He sighs contentedly when I find some good spots that need attention. Dogs demand our undivided attention. They want to be petted until they are satisfied, not when you think you are done.

Because dogs live in the moment, we must learn to relate to our dogs in terms of moments. My dog does not care about what I did yesterday by holding grudges or what I am going to do in the future, all he wants of me is my present-moment attention. The other morning my dog wanted his morning present-moment attention before I got out of bed. I normally just jump out of bed and start my day. He has gotten me to slow down and focus on just him and not what I have to be doing in a few minutes. He has forced me to enjoy the moment of feeling his soft fur and just relaxing for a while before I head out to work. Our little petting session relaxes me and makes me calmer and ready for another day. We all need to be more like dogs, become one with what we love and enjoy the ride.

Learn to STOP, SEE, UNDERSTAND, and CHOOSE!

Why is mindfulness important in our professions as correctional educators? The practice of mindfulness slows us down and makes us more aware of our surroundings so we can add to a safe work environment. Mindfulness also helps us become more self-aware. We are more confident about our work. We are more alert to our own strengths and weaknesses.

How can we practice mindfulness at work? The first step is to become aware. Awareness of anything is the first step. Did you know that our brain processes over 400 billion bits of information, yet we are only aware of 2 billion bits? When we are aware of a problem in our lives then we can cognitively choose to do something about it. Awareness is important in any work setting. There are regulations that promote awareness. For instance, there is a Public Law, "The Computer Security Act of 1987," which mandated the creation of guidance on computer security awareness. There is also a publication titled, *Building an Information Technology Security Awareness and Training Program*. There are courses in Cultural Awareness, Workplace Safety Awareness, Drug Awareness, Domestic Violence Awareness, Team Awareness, Legal Awareness, Latex Awareness, and Mental Health Awareness. There seems to be awareness training everywhere we look.

We need to be aware of what we are or are not doing. In a correctional setting we can't just go around mindlessly doing our business. When we unlock our doors we must also be aware that we need to lock it. When we use our keys, we need to be aware of where they are at all times. In our classrooms we need to be aware of the other students in relation to where we are. All our senses must be aware in the correctional setting.

The next step is to slow down and try not to multi-task. I realize that we as correctional educators are constantly multi-tasking. If we are aware that we are doing several tasks at once then we should also be able to let go of this habit. We need to be able to focus our attention on our surroundings and do one thing at a time.

Mindfulness or awareness can be practiced anywhere and is an important practice in our profession. Our jobs require us to be mindful in order to make it safe for those who work with us. The first step to being mindful is awareness of our actions and surroundings. By being aware of our actions, we can better protect ourselves and the people who work with us and around us.

Activity:

At work practice mindfulness by slowing down several times a day. When you get in to work pay attention to your classroom or work area. Did you leave something unlocked the night before? Did you leave something out that should have been locked away? During the day use your keys as a reminder to focus on small but important tasks. When you hold your keys be aware and focus on locking your door when you leave the room. Let the jangle of your keys remind you to log off the computer. Focus on your desk and the paperwork it contains. Did you remember to shred that secure document? Did you secure the student file you were working on? Did you throw out the top of the soup can into the hot trash? When preparing to leave work, instead of focusing on getting home, focus on locking the file cabinets, logging off your computer, closing the windows, putting tools away, locking the door behind you. Then you can focus on getting home safely.

Not only can mindfulness help you at work and in your personal life, but it also helps us to become more in tune to the universe. Being in the present moment develops synchronicity. The definition of synchronicity, according to Jung himself, is a meaningful coincidence. For instance, I may be reading a book with the television or radio on. I read a word and at the same time I read that word I hear it on the radio or television. Another time I am listening to the television and scrolling down the guide when I hear a word and at the same time I see the word in the guide. And yet another occasion I am reading something and my husband says the same exact phrase I just read. When you are in the present moment you become more attuned to the interconnectedness of things in your life.

Being in the present moment can also enhance your workouts even if you aren't working out. Through the use of visualization, one can workout better. In a study at Bishop's University, some athletes were told to mentally train a body part only, others were told to use visualization and physically train the same body part, and others were told to do no training, physically or mentally of the same body part. The ones who only trained using visualization showed a 24% increase in their physical strength. The athletes who both visually and physically trained showed a 28% increase in strength while the ones who did nothing showed no significant changes. Visualizing is all about being completely entrenched in the moment.

Activity:

Buddhists practice mindfulness by walking very slowly so they can feel every step their feet make. While walking mindfully, attention is paid to the feelings the body is experiencing. The senses are heightened because the focus is on one thing at a time. Time essentially slows down. Go outside and find a place to walk. It doesn't have to be a big area or many miles, or even a quiet spot. Start by walking very slowly, one step at a time. Pay attention to the little things, like how your feet feel, how your breathing changes, the unevenness of the ground. Feel each step that you take. How does your foot strike? What part touches the ground first? Listen to what is going on around you. Feel the sun or the breeze. What do you smell? How do you feel? (You may feel a little off balance doing this exercise because it causes you to really slow down your gait.)

Activity:

Another way to practice mindfulness is to observe your surroundings. Lie down next to a pond or a river or even just lay on the grass. Look up to the sky and see what the water or grass sees, feel the breeze the water and grass feels. Observe the birds that quench their thirst at the water's edge. Observe the birds which fly overhead. Watch the clouds that float by. Feel and see what the water or grass is experiencing. Slow down and become aware.

Activity:

This is a way to establish a simple and physical connection with present reality. Try it for yourself, right now. Look around you. Listen. What do you hear? Make contact with things around you. Touch your spouse, feel the hard wood of your desk, touch the pages of this book. Smell the air. What do you smell? Whatever happened long ago, whatever happened in the recent past, whatever will happen is not your present concern. This moment is all you have to worry about. If you can focus your attention to this moment you can reconnect with the here and now. This is also a useful exercise if you experience panic attacks. Focusing on what you are doing in the moment during a panic attack will alleviate what you are feeling because you are focusing on the here and now.

Activity:

Be aware of what you say. In my job with the military as a Public Affairs Officer we have to work around real world media. When asked questions by the press, we cannot just blurt out whatever we think. We have to mindfully think about what we are going to say. Because whatever we say, once it is out there, we can't take it back. Try slowing down before speaking. Pause before each sentence. This slight pause gives you the opportunity to consider and evaluate mindfully the content of your next thoughts. What is the intent of your words? Do you want to help someone or hurt someone? Can you find better words of kindness or compassion? Do you really want to say what you are about to say? Before engaging the tongue, engage the mind. Practice speaking with mindfulness.

Activity:
Start the day with a time of silence. Start your day connecting to your inner energy and strength. Practice "mind over mattress" and get up a little earlier to give you some breathing space before the hustle of the day. So many of us hear the alarm and grumble that we have to get up and go to work. Why not hear the alarm and be overjoyed that we have another opportunity to live a full life. *Today, be aware of how you are spending your 86,400 beautiful moments, and spend them wisely.*

Waking up I smile. Twenty-four brand new hours are before me. I vow to live fully in each moment. ~ Thich Nhat Hanh

*Go back and reread the checklist at the beginning of the chapter. Have your thoughts changed?

YOU DON'T NEED TO DO IT ALL.

What actually happened?
The teacher did not know that the offenders had taken pictures of old pornographic magazines that were supposed to have been confiscated several years earlier. They were making copies and passing them around the institution.

What should the teacher have done?
1. *The teacher should have stopped trying to do it all.*
2. *He should have only chosen to do a few things rather than do too many things at once.*
3. *The education supervisor should have also intervened earlier by asking if he was taking on too much at once or telling him to choose to only do a few things.*

Chapter 4

THINK POSITIVE, STAY FOCUSED AND MOTIVATED

SEND THE MONEY OR THEY WILL BEAT ME UP

The offender needed a lot of attention and was constantly getting into trouble. The teacher was always providing him guidance. Once the inmate talked about hurting himself so the teacher thought she should give him some extra consideration. One day, the offender told the teacher that he owed some money to some bad guys who were going to give him the beating of his life. The offender asked her if she could send some money to his ex wife so she could pay them off. The teacher was not sure what to do. The offender told her, "Oh come on. You can send the money." Then he gave the name and address of his ex wife. All the teacher had to do was send a money order and no one would know anything.

What happened and what would you do? (See end of chapter.)

THINK POSITIVE, STAY FOCUSED AND MOTIVATED

Before you read this section think about the following statements.
Mark each statement:

A for agree
D for disagree
? if you are undecided

1. I have not grown in my profession.	
2. I make sure I attend conferences each year.	
3. I have attended education courses since I received my last degree.	
4. I always try to improve myself and my teaching when I can.	
5. I think it is important to belong to professional organizations.	
6. I feel reading professional journals helps me in my profession.	
7. I share what works in my classroom with fellow educators.	
8. I think writing for professional publications about my profession is important.	
9. I set realistic goals for myself.	
10. As I meet my goals I try and make more ambitious ones.	
11. When I feel less motivated I try something new or different.	
12. I try to find inspiration in what other teachers are doing.	
13. When I don't feel motivated I allow my standards to drop.	
14. I always try to see the value in what I am doing.	
15. I take advantage of all that my job has to offer.	

16. I reward myself.	
17. I am adaptable.	
18. I am proactive.	
19. I never allow myself to become complacent.	
20. I realized that life is not perfect and accept it.	
21. I seek out opportunities to do more.	
22. I try to stay enthusiastic and positive.	
23. I maintain a healthy work/life balance.	
24. I try to surround myself with positive people.	
25. I plan my day.	
26. I take breaks when I need to.	
27. I give myself something to look forward to.	
28. I have someone I can talk to when I am not feeling motivated or positive.	

Eat a live frog first thing in the morning and nothing worse can happen to you. ~ *An Old Saying*

Do you wish that you could stay focused, motivated and keep a positive attitude at all time? You know that feeling that you get and feel when have just come out of a great seminar at a conference. You feel so pumped up. You are ready to get back into your classroom and do fantastic things with your students. You have tons of ideas, you are excited and you can't wait to get back to work. After a couple of days that feeling fades and eventually melts away until the reality of life gets in the way. That's when you need to tell yourself to think positive despite the challenges of your everyday life.

There are many times that we have to grapple with things that are happening in our lives and then we still have to show up for work in a positive frame of mind. We have deaths occur in our family, someone falls ill that we must take care of, we go through divorces, or perhaps we are the ones who are suffering from an illness. How do we deal with what is going on in our lives yet come to work as if everything is finer than frog's hair?

Other times, our motivation lags not because of what is going on in our personal lives but in our classrooms. For instance, I teach an ESL class two times a week in the evenings. Those evenings occur on my long day. My long day starts out at 4:30 in the morning when I teach a fitness class outside prison and continues on until 9 in the evening. My ESL students are Hispanic. None are U.S. citizens so they will all be eventually deported. They work in the kitchen all day and then eat dinner and come immediately to class. They don't want to be there. They don't want to learn English because they are going back to Mexico. They see no point in working on their education. They are tired and they are cranky. This is what I have to look forward to. I have tried different things to motivate them because I blame myself for their lack of motivation. I even attended a one-month, 12-credit *Teaching English as a Second Language* Graduate Intensive Course in hopes I would learn something to help me with my students. I finally realized that even if I stand on my head and do somersaults, I can't save everyone. I can't blame myself for what is not happening with my students. I have to accept the fact that there will be some students who really want to learn and there will be others who choose to vegetate. I still come to work every day with hopes that I can make a difference for someone, and that is what keeps me going. I still have faith in my abilities to teach. Don't lose faith in yourself and what you are capable of. You must also have hope that all your students are capable of making something of themselves. You must have hope that what you do makes a difference in their lives even if you don't see the outcome, because if you have hope in your students they will have hope in themselves.

Some days, not all days, we just have this feeling that we can't quite put our finger on. We feel disenchanted. Maybe it is because the day before, some of the offenders were blaming you for their lack of learning. I am sure we have all heard an offender say, "I am not learning anything in here. You aren't teaching me." "Move me out of your class because you aren't working with me enough." "You are always working with those other students and don't spend any time with me." These types of comments can be draining and disparaging if we dwell on them and let the comments get the better of us. Other times we may look at the students and think of the movie "Groundhog Day." "I keep going over and over the same things with these guys and it just doesn't seem to stick. Is this what it is going to be like my whole career?" So sometimes we don't feel as thrilled about going to work as we normally do. It is during times like these that we must reach deep inside ourselves and find something to grasp and hold onto to keep us going.

I don't know how many of you reading this have ever run a marathon, walked a very long distance, or hiked up a steep mountain. If you have you would know all there is to staying focused and motivated. When you do things that really stress your body and push you beyond your personal limits you learn the importance of staying focused and motivated. You learn to always keep looking ahead and never look back. You focus on what you can do right now. You set small attainable goals each mile rather than looking at the total distance you still have left. You sustain yourself to keep your energy up and your body moving. You know when to slow down or take some breaks to keep fresh. You have positive conversations with yourself; no negative self-talk. You don't think about the next race, just what you have to accomplish now. You look forward to finishing not winning. You never doubt yourself because you know you put in a lot of miles, hours, training, and hard work to get where you are. And the most important of all, you just keep going.

How to Keep Fresh and Motivated in Your Profession
Here are some ways you can keep your job fresh and stimulating.

Envision yourself as a Verb instead of a Noun
Do you see yourself as a noun? We tend to label ourselves as nouns. I am a teacher, a mother, a father, a nurse, a woman, or a man. Why not try to view yourself as a verb. When you start picturing yourself as what you do and not what you are, you open yourself up to tremendous possibilities. I am not just a teacher but I am creative, disciplined, colorful, active, a go-getter, intelligent, and demanding. Describe yourself using verbs. Who are you? What do you do? Do your possibilities increase when you see yourself as a verb or verbs? Do you have more choices as a verb?

Advance your professional growth.
Are you teaching using the most current and accurate information because you constantly pursue new information and updates? As educators we must have an insatiable curiosity about the world around us. If you stop learning, you die — or at least you won't grow in our profession. I know they say that prostitution is the oldest profession, but teaching is right up there. Just because it is one of the oldest professions doesn't mean that teaching is stagnant. Things are happening — old methods are breaking down and new methods are forming. Because our profession is in a constant state of renewal, it also means that what I teach today may change tomorrow! Just like our students, you have to learn by doing. Immerse and throw yourself completely into your profession. You have to enrich your own lives through formal or informal learning activities.

How? Get off your butt, attend conferences and workshops, go back to school, join professional organizations, write for professional publication, and participate in the correctional education culture. If teaching is not your passion anymore, then rethink why you're doing this and consider doing something else.

Strive for professional diversity.

You may have gotten a degree in teaching but as you grow and mature in your profession, think about additional training and experience that will allow you to go boldly where you have never been before. Branch out and try new things. Get a specialization certificate in another area of teaching. Volunteer to present at conferences. Share your knowledge with others by writing or training others. Get out there and do something different. Stretch your wings, reinvent yourself, and get out of your comfort zone. The definition of a comfort zone is a set of environments and behaviors with which one is comfortable, without creating a sense of risk. How boring is that! No wonder you are not motivated anymore.

Do you establish personal and professional goals? Do you work to attain those goals? If you don't, here is how to get started:

Set S.M.A.R.T.Goals.
S: Specific
M: Measurable
A: Attainable
R: Realistic/Rewarded
T: Timed

Specific goals are based on an action and are narrowly focused. Don't choose several things to work on when setting a goal. Pick only one area you want to change. For example, "I want to lose weight by walking."

Measurable goals need criteria to assess change and track progress. Measurable goals are like setting objectives for a classroom lesson. What are you going to measure? For example, "I want to lose 10 pounds by walking."

Attainable goals are appropriate, short-term, planned, broken into small steps, time defined, and not overwhelming. If you want to lose weight, don't set a goal of losing ten pounds in two weeks. A goal of two pounds a week is attainable not two pounds a day. Don't set goals that so overwhelm you that you want to quit.

Realistic goals don't set you up for failure. You need to under-promise and over-deliver. You must be willing and able to work toward these goals. Be honest about what you can do and be positive; don't expect perfection and don't be so hard on yourself when you slip. It happens to everyone. Pick yourself up and continue on your journey.

Successful goals are rewarded. Celebrate your successes and make the celebrations meaningful to you. Keep the rewards simple yet enjoyable. Make sure your rewards are appropriate to your goal. Reward yourself with a new workout shirt or shorts. Maybe get a subscription to a health magazine, not an order of nacho cheese fries.

Finally, successful goals are timed. Establish a timeline for starting and completing your goals. For example a short-term goal may be, "I want to lose 2 pounds a week this month." A medium term goal may be, "I want to lose 20 pounds in the next 3 months starting January 1st." A long-term goal would look like, "I want to lose 48 pounds by June 20th so I can fit in my wedding dress."

Activity:

Write down one goal that you want to achieve. Make sure it's S.M.A.R.T and make sure you include a reward!

Activity:

Each time a negative thought surfaces, catch yourself and write down your negative self-talk. Then replace the negative statement with a positive one. After writing down your positive self-talk, verbalize the new positive self-talk so you can keep reinforcing these positive thought patterns. One way to do this is look in the mirror every morning and repeat your positive thought several times. Do this several times a day even without a mirror.

NEGATIVE SELF-TALK	POSITIVE SELF-TALK
I have no time to exercise.	I am going to bring my tennis shoes to work so I can walk during lunch.

Activity:

If your mind is like a car then you must "carefully drive" it. What do you need to drive the "car" well? What does the car look like? What does the road look like? Are you alone in the car? Where did you get your driving lessons? Are there any driving habits you wish you could change? Draw a picture of your mind as a car.

Go back and reread the checklist at the beginning of the chapter. Have your thoughts changed?

SEND THE MONEY OR THEY WILL BEAT ME UP

What actually happened?

The teacher in this situation actually sent a 50-dollar money order and later lost her job.

The teacher should have done:

1. Brought up concerns about this offender to other staff before it got out of hand.
2. Documented questionable behavior.
3. Called the counselor to report that the offender was thinking about hurting himself.
4. Reported the conversation to her supervisor.

Chapter 5

WORKING WITH DIFFICULT PEOPLE

GAINING CONFIDENCE

   An offender used the teacher's religion to gain confidence. She brought her bible to school and would read it while the students read their own books. The offender would ask her if he could read her bible because he didn't have one. She let him use the bible in class. She never gave a second thought to the highlighted parts that were important to her. He would later use this for conversations starters. He asked her questions about her personal life. She gave him the address of family members and their phone numbers. This went on for quite a bit. Then he started making comments about having a relationship with her. Their hands would brush as she passed out papers. Finally after three months, he asked her for money.

What happened and what would you do? (See end of chapter.)

WORKING WITH DIFFICULT PEOPLE

Before you read this section think about the following statements.
Mark each statement:

A for agree
D for disagree
? if you are undecided

1. I grind my teeth in frustration each time I have to work closely with someone who drives me batty.	
2. I put up with difficult people at work on a regular basis.	
3. My physician has told me that my blood pressure is high.	
4. I take things personally.	
5. The angrier my thoughts become, the angrier I become.	
6. I react without thinking.	
7. I always have to be right.	
8. It's my way or the highway.	
9. The way I perceive things is based on my reality.	
10. The way others perceive things is based on their reality.	
11. I feel supported by the correctional officers I work with.	
12. I feel at odds with the correctional officers I work with.	
13. It has nothing to do with me.	
14. Most people have positive intentions.	
15. I feel uncomfortable bringing up how I feel.	

16. I listen to all viewpoints.	
17. I don't dwell on the past.	
18. I let things go.	
19. I avoid instinctive reactions.	
20. I avoid issues.	
21. I jump in without assessing or understanding the problem.	
22. I control myself so others don't.	
23. I treat others with unconditional respect.	
24. I let small annoying behaviors of others go unattended.	
25. I avoid gossip.	
26. I am able to recognize that I have contributed to a problem.	
27. I am able to seek help from others for my own problems.	
28. I am able to set behavioral limits and consequences.	
29. I remember the good things.	

Be kind to unkind people - they need it the most
  ~ Ashleigh Brilliant

Difficult people come in every conceivable variety. Some talk constantly and never listen to what we have to say. Others must always have the last word. Some coworkers fail to keep commitments or are never on time. Others criticize anything and everything but have no solutions. Difficult coworkers compete with you for power, privilege and the spotlight. Some talk behind your back and others just want to talk about what is going on in their lives. A few are highly argumentative, some just ramble on and on, and some don't say much at all. Sound familiar? How many of these folks do you encounter at work? Maybe you are one of these people. We all have been difficult at one time or another. Many of our difficulties are minor and those are sometimes the hardest to recognize and address. What can you do about difficult people in your life? You have two options: You can believe there are difficult people or you can believe there are no difficult people - just opportunities.

First, if you believe that there are difficult people, are they really being difficult or are you just blowing it out of proportion? Ask yourself:
1. Does this person have a history of being a difficult person?
2. If there is a history, how far back does it go?
3. If there isn't a history of difficult behavior, is this person reacting to a particular event?
4. If so, is this event work-related or of a personal nature?
5. After self-evaluation, does it appear that I'm overreacting to this person?
6. What issues or biases do I have that could be prejudicing me toward this person?
7. I wonder what his or her story is.
8. What else is going on?

STRATEGIES FOR COPING WITH DIFFICULT PEOPLE
The Plan:
How many times after dealing with a difficult person have you thought: "It is easier to get mad and hide out at home and be mad at people and not like them. That way I don't have to engage or be

62

challenged. I don't have to go up to the person I am mad at and say what is bothering me about the relationship or apologize." Or, "Why didn't I handle that better?" Or, "I should have said something different." If this happens to you, then you need to plan ahead for coping with difficult people. Take into consideration the type of person you are dealing with, the behaviors that this person exhibits, and how you will cope with this person. Just like in anything you do, you should make a plan, review your plan, and practice your plan.

The Army calls it an after action review. Personal trainers call it a food journal. A study published in the August 2008 issue of the *American Journal of Preventive Medicine* found that keeping a food log can actually double a person's weight loss. Writing down what you eat puts your food habits in perspective. Likewise, writing down what you did and said puts your behaviors in perspective. Whatever you call it, it is a way to see what you are doing in black and white. Write down what happened. What did the other person do? What did you do? How did that person act? What did they say? How did you act? What did you say? Now look at what you wrote. What could you have done or said differently that would have made a difference.

Now make a plan based on what you can do differently to change the situation. If you trust someone's judgment, have them look at your plan.

Now practice it. Runners go over the race route in their heads. Athletes go over what they are going to do during a game or event. Do the same thing. Practice it in your head. If you have to, say the words you will say out loud. The key is to practice.

Now commit yourself to the plan. Tell yourself that the next time you engage this person you will follow your plan and stick to it. Remember, be open to outcome rather than attached to it.

AND WHAT ABOUT YOU?

Is it always about you?

If it is not about you then what is it about?

It's all about ATTITUDE!

You are not going to change THEM.

You have no control over THEM.

You will have to work with THEM.

You can't take things personally.

You are the one who can make the change.

Make it happen!

Gather Information
1. Get the facts. You should be objective.
2. Put yourself in the others person's shoes. What do you think they are thinking or feeling? This means that we must be mindful of the kinds of interpretations we are making of others' behavior and speech.
3. What are my opinions and beliefs about this person? What is it I think is true and what do I believe is actually happening.
4. What is it that I want to come out of this situation? In other words, what is your goal? Keep it simple, realistic and positive.

Remember - everyone seems normal... until you get to know them.
  ~ Seen on a bumper sticker

Expect the Best from People
    What do you expect from yourself? The best I hope. What do you expect from your loved ones? Again, the answer would be the best. Then why do you expect something different from difficult people? You usually expect the worst. I have done this many times. A new offender comes into my class who complains about everything. He doesn't want to be in school, why is the Department of Corrections (DOC) forcing him to take classes. So right away the "expect the worst radar is up." The offender gets up to leave with the rest of the students who have to leave class early to go to work. Right away, I

think he is lying. I am ready to write him up. But first I call someone to see if he actually works. Sure enough, he is on a call-out for work. I then think to myself, why did I assume he was going to lie? I was expecting the worst from him. I have to reframe how I look at difficult offenders. I have to expect the best from them and erase my negative expectations. Sometimes you have to look at things from their point of view. Are they really trying to be difficult on purpose or are they legitimately upset. Meet people where they are at.

Another way to look at the difficult person is to look at them with compassion. The Dalai Lama says to treat people with compassion. I know it is difficult to look with compassion at an offender who is aggravating you at the time. Try it. Think positive thoughts about the person and send those thoughts to them. Instead of reacting negatively think positively. Once the offender or person exhibits the behavior you want to see, reinforce that behavior. Draw attention to that positive behavior. So many times, these difficult people have never had anybody expect the best from them, so they never expected the best from themselves. Now is your opportunity to help them to expect the best.

Now, there are many, many people in the world, but relatively few with whom we interact, and even fewer who cause us problems. So, when you come across such a chance for practicing patience and tolerance, you should treat it with gratitude. It is rare. Just as having unexpectedly found a treasure in your own house, you should be happy and grateful to your enemy for providing that precious opportunity. ~ Dalai Lama

Activity:
Get a sheet of paper and at the top, title it with the person's name.
· Make a list of every positive aspect you can think of.
· When you think you are done, keep going. Write down even the tiniest thing.
· Now read through your list at least 5 times.
· Review your list before you encounter the person again. Notice what's changed.
· Keep practicing!

Remember, we are all shareholders so we all affect the bottom line. We all have an effect on the company or the success of our education department, so we should try to lift each other up, working together to make a positive environment.

Remember to **BREATHE**:
Be mindful and collaborative
Recognize others as being valuable
Every person has something to contribute
Attentively listen
Take time for kindness
Honor our differences
Engage in continuous and open communication

*Go back and reread the checklist at the beginning of the chapter. Have your thoughts changed?

GAINING CONFIDENCE

What happened?
1. The teacher reported the offender for asking her for money.
2. She turned in her letter of resignation.

What should the teacher have done?
1. Be empathetic rather than sympathetic. Although the terms empathy and sympathy are often tossed into one terminological bag, they should be distinguished in working with offenders. Both concepts involve sharing, but empathetic teachers share their understanding, while sympathetic teachers share their emotions with the offender.
2. The teacher should have paid attention to lending the offender her Bible, especially when she highlighted sections of it. Unlike highlighting important points in a book, highlighting things in the bible often indicate very personal things that are important to us.
3. I don't know why she gave him the address of her family members and their phone numbers. Maybe she thought they could help him if the offender was trying to come across as religious. Regardless of what he was trying to do, she should never have given out personal information about herself or her family.
4. When the offender started making comments about having a relationship with her she should have reported that immediately after telling him those comments were inappropriate. By letting their hands brush as she passed out papers she was basically letting the offender know it was okay for them to have a relationship.
5. If she had reported the comments about a relationship earlier, the set-up would not have gone as far as it did. By the time she reported the offender for asking her for money, she felt it was too late to fix anything so she turned in her letter of resignation.

Chapter 6

STRESS MANAGEMENT

NEW TEACHER

A new teacher had been working at her job for about 90 days. She would have students work at her desk individually after they did a group work lesson. One student who worked at her desk would keep covering his mouth when he talked. She finally asked why he did this. He said he had bad breath, didn't have any money to buy toothpaste. The teacher felt sorry for him so she brought in toothpaste for the offender. Then the offender started asking for more items to be brought in. He told her if she didn't bring in what he asked for he would tell on her. He asked her to bring in a cell phone. She started bringing in pieces of a cell phone. She actually knew what she was doing was wrong. She just felt it was too late to do anything about it. She thought she would lose her job anyway, so why stop. So she kept bringing in more things.

What happened and what would you do? (See end of chapter.)

STRESS MANAGEMENT

Before you read this section think about the following statements.
Mark each statement:

> **A** for agree
> **D** for disagree
> **?** if you are undecided

1. Working in prison affects my interpersonal relationships with my loved ones.	
2. I feel myself caught in a triangle of correctional officers, the offenders, and myself.	
3. I take my work home with me.	
4. My work at prison is always on my mind.	
5. I work out at least three days a week for 30 minutes.	
6. I save money and have little financial worries.	
7. I have someone I can talk to about problems.	
8. I am not afraid of seeking outside counseling help.	
9. I am spiritual. (You may be religious or not.)	
10. I get at least eight hours a sleep at night.	
11. I follow a healthy diet with plenty of vegetables, fruit, and fiber.	
12. I watch my intake of caffeine.	
13. I am kind to myself.	
14. I let go of things that bother me rather than holding on to them.	
15. I know how to relax.	

16. I feel I have a balanced life.	
17. I rarely get sick.	
18. I take vitamin supplements.	
19. I drink alcohol in moderation.	
20. I try to live in the moment.	
21. I don't smoke.	
22. My daily schedule is overwhelming.	
23. I have little control at work or in my life.	
24. I know how to create peaceful times in my day.	
25. I am organized at home and at work.	

I consider myself an expert on love, sex, and health. Without health you can have very little of the other two.
  ~ *Barbara Cartland*

When my father was dying of Alzheimer's two years ago, I went to visit him in the hospital. He was sitting in a wheelchair looking frail and weak, his hair a little disheveled. He had been through a lot in the last few months. His wonderful and active mind had been deteriorating for years now. He would get so frustrated because he could not remember things. He would repeat himself many times. My father had lost his mother at a very young age. He had been in the Korean and Vietnam Wars. He suffered through kidney and skin cancer. Now he was battling dementia. Before I left to go back home, I hugged and held onto him. I started crying because I knew in my heart this would be my last goodbye. I always looked toward my father for advice and even now, when his mind didn't always work quite right, my father still had words of wisdom to impart to me. My father bent his head toward my ear and whispered these cherished last words, "Go with the flow." I was so surprised he said these words because he was never a man to "go with the flow." Nevertheless, I keep these words engraved on my heart. Every time things start getting crazy, I remember his last words.

You can't get uptight about things that happen. You can't always change things that happen to you. You can always go with the flow. Just go with what happens and embrace it, don't fight it. Don't stress out over everything that happens in your life. Accept it and move on. Stressing will not change things or make anything different. Stressing just makes you sick. It doesn't mean that the stress in our lives is going to go away, but the way we face our stress might change. Going with the flow makes you stronger. Look at the trees that have endured storms. They are permanently bent a certain way because that is how the wind blew. They are still around. The trees that failed to bend with storms snapped and no longer exist. The river does not fight its path; it flows around obstacles and keeps going. Remember, when things are tough, go with the flow.

As a lecturer once described stress management to an audience, stress is like holding a glass of water for way too long. The longer you hold it, the heavier it becomes. The water weight is still the same but if you keep holding on to it, you will eventually drop it. At some point you will need to set it down and take a break.

Stress is harmful to people if we carry it around too long and it is harmful if we internalize it. Glass is no exception. Glass should be as strong as steal if it isn't suffering from internal stress. Because of the nature of its atomic bonds, glass should be about five times as strong as steel. However, glass tends to have less strength than we think. One of the main reasons for its loss of strength is surface and internal stress. If glass is cooled too rapidly, high stresses are "frozen" inside, and may cause the piece to simply shatter. To avoid these internal stresses, glass articles must be annealed. In the annealing process, the temperature of the object is raised to that which will allow the internal stress to be relaxed.

Stress is a fact of life and a condition of employment for correctional educators. To some people, even our loved ones, teaching in a prison does not seem stressful. Much of our stress is due to our heightened level of awareness and watchfulness. We are always scanning our environment for changes, clues that something may happen. Sometimes we face difficulties in adjusting to a work environment where our services are considered subordinate to the primary mission of the correctional setting, which is security. We have the dual challenge of adjusting what our role is as supportive educators without interfering with security in a corrections setting. We also have to maintain a professional rapport with our students, which creates a tension high wire that is difficult to navigate.

The correctional environment is a chronically stressful one. Studies done by Frances Cheek indicate that the life expectancy of a correctional officer is only 59 years, compared to 78 years for the average American. Correctional educators don't have to be around a lot of the stressors in the cell blocks as correctional officers do, but we still have plenty of stress because we are around the students six to eight hours a day. We have students who don't want to do anything, and so that is what they do - nothing. We have students who don't want to do anything but make trouble and disrupt the classroom.

We also have a lot of mentally ill offenders in the classroom. More than half of all prison and state inmates now report mental health problems, including symptoms of major depression, mania and psychotic disorders, according to a Federal Bureau of Justice Statistics (BJS) report. Each day, correctional educators must contend with offenders with little or no information about the offender's histories, degrees of violence, crimes, and so on.

The correctional environment is also very unpredictable. Correctional educators have to deal with many interruptions in the classroom. Correctional officers' barge into the classroom while you are teaching a class, go straight to a student, cuff him and take him out. You are left standing there with your adrenaline going and upset students. Maybe a fight will break out and you have to call out for help. Another time officers will come in shouting that there is a recall count and everyone has to clear out of the building. Or maybe officers roam the hallways checking to see who is not following the clothing policy in the building. Officers come in and tell students to take off their hats, tuck in their shirts, pull up their pants, or go back to their cell and put the right shirt on. Maybe a rape occurs and you have to shut down education operations. During all of these events you are trying to teach a lesson or keep some semblance of order in your classroom. Unpredictability can cause heightened levels of employee stress. Anyone who works in a correctional environment must acquire a heightened level of awareness. Prepare for it and deal with it by having a healthy well-balanced life outside. If you need to talk, find someone away from work to offer counsel.

Educators constantly give but rarely receive. This is even truer in a correctional setting. We rarely receive feedback on what we are doing right but we sure know when we are doing something wrong. There are so many expected role behaviors that are inconsistent and a lack of clear, consistent information regarding our duties and responsibilities within the corrections setting. An unstable work environment, where workers are unsure of their roles and lack clear communication, increases the risk of heart attack, according to a study by Finnish researchers from the Finnish Institute of Occupational Health published in *The American Journal of Public Health.*

The absence of a good support group, that is, our educational co-workers, adds to job stress and eventually burnout. If we don't have a strong educational support group to provide emotional comfort, confront us when our behaviors are inappropriate, encourage individual growth, serve as a sounding board, and share similar values and beliefs, then we won't stand a chance in our environment. The same goes for a social support network outside of education.

Activity:

Below, list some people who will be part of your social support network and the ways they can support you.

Person/Relationship	Ways they can support
1.	1.
2.	2.
3.	3.
4.	4.

When we keep giving of ourselves and don't refill our emotional jar we eventually find ourselves running on empty. We can't let ourselves get tapped out. We must do the things that offer physical, emotional and spiritual nourishment. That means self-nurture or putting you first! If this sounds too selfish then reword it: take care of yourself like those you love and tend to.

Many people think taking care of themselves is frivolous. They can take care of others, but not themselves. But if we don't take care of our business, who will? It is not selfish to do what allows us to continue giving to others. It is not selfish to treat ourselves with the same thoughtfulness we show others. Taking care of our business is like making a date with ourselves. When you make a date with someone, you usually really care about them and want the relationship to blossom. Taking the time to workout and eat healthy is making a date with yourself. If you keep breaking that date you must not really love yourself. Date yourself more often.

As a personal trainer, wellness coach, and kettlebell and fit camp instructor, I can tell you that there are a lot of pieces to the puzzle in preventing stress, exhaustion, and sickness. Exercise is one of the best things you can do for yourself. I would say diet is next, then sleep, and finally keeping your mind still with relaxation.

If I were to tell you that by doing this one thing several times a week, you would gain more energy, you wouldn't need that cup of java every day, you would sleep better, get sick less, lose weight, lower your dental bills, and prevent blindness later on in life, would you do it? What is this secret to a better life? Exercise!

Get plenty of exercise. The studies that show the benefits of exercise are overwhelming. Exercise reduces stress, improves your mood, helps you lose weight, promotes better sleep, lowers blood pressure and cholesterol, combats chronic disease, strengthens your heart and lungs, leaves you feeling energized, and fights aging. You have absolutely nothing to lose by exercising. It is one of the single most effective ways to improve your health overall.

As a personal trainer and wellness coach, I can't tell you enough how important exercise is. I constantly see clients coming in who before exercising were always tired, felt sluggish, and were overweight and out of shape. Once these same clients started exercising they could fit in their clothes, they had more energy, and felt so much better overall.

People who exercise also use less sick days. In a study in the *Canadian Journal of Public Health*, physical activity appears to reduce the risk for over 25 chronic conditions, in particular coronary heart disease, stroke, hypertension, breast cancer, colon cancer, type-2 diabetes, and osteoporosis. Employees who regularly do exercise are less likely to take time off work because their immune system tends to improve. In fact, exercise can slash your cold risk by 33 percent according to a study at the University of Washington. Exercise helps your body fight off cold bugs and other germs. Women ages 50 to 75 who did 45 minutes of cardio, five days a week, had a third as many colds as those who did once-weekly stretching sessions. Research also shows that people who participate in vigorous leisure-time physical activity just once or twice a week take about half the sick time of those who are more sedentary. Another study by the University of Bristol recently showed exercise helped to reenergize and improve concentration and helped people feel calmer and happier at work. On days staffers participated in on-site fitness activities, they reported thinking more clearly, getting more done, and interacting more effectively with colleagues.

Did you know that exercise can lower your dental bills? Mohammad

Al-Zahrani, D.D.S., Ph.D., a former associate professor at Case Western Reserve University, says that exercise plays an important role in dental health. In a study, Al-Zahrani discovered that adults who did 30 minutes of moderate activity five or more times a week were 42 percent less likely to suffer from periodontal disease.

Having trouble sleeping? Say goodnight to poor sleep because exercise can help you sleep better. According to a study in *Sleep Medicine*, women age 60 and older who walked or danced for at least an hour, four times a week, woke up half as often and slept an average 48 minutes more a night than sedentary women.

Physical activity is not only good for your heart but it is good for your eyes. An active lifestyle can cut your risk of age-related macular degeneration by up to 70 percent, according to a *British Journal of Ophthalmology* study of 4,000 adults. Macular degeneration is the most common cause of blindness in people after age 60.

Exercise can help you enjoy instant energy. If you're among the 50 percent of adults who report feeling tired at least one day a week and drink coffee to give you a pick up, skip the caffeine and go for a walk. University of Georgia researchers concluded that moving your body increases energy and reduces fatigue. This is important, just moving your body. Not just sweating, but heart-pumping workouts will produce these effects. Regular exercise boosts certain fatigue-fighting brain chemicals such as norepinephrine and dopamine, which pep you up, and serotonin, a mood enhancer.

Exercise is not the only thing you must do. You also must watch what you eat. Food, when eaten the way it should be, is like gasoline for your car. How many of you won't put anything but high-test gasoline in your cars? If you won't pump low-grade gasoline into your car, then why would you do that to your body? Food should be eaten to help you do what you need to do every day. It should be eaten to energize you, repair you, nourish you; not overfeed you.

Be aware of what you eat. Stay away from too many sugars and processed foods. Eat several small meals throughout the day. If you eat large meals you will feel sleepy. You don't have to go on a diet, just eat in moderation.

Eat carbohydrates, fats, and proteins. Many people think carbohydrates are bad. Carbohydrates are not the enemy. You need carbohydrates to keep your brain functioning. When you cut out all carbohydrates you will feel dizzy, lethargic, and may suffer from very bad breath. Here is a great website to keep you straight on your diet and exercise: http://caloriecount.about.com. It is an online pie hole diary (food diary) that tells you how many calories you should eat for maintenance and how many calories you need to lose weight and a weight loss date. It also allows you to input what you eat and your activities then gives you a report on calories, carbohydrates, fats, protein, sugars and how many calories you burn from your workouts. IT IS FREE! Check it out!

Don't deprive yourself. Take time when you eat. Don't eat standing up or while multi-tasking. Eating while multitasking, whether working through lunch or watching TV, often leads us to eat more because we eat mindlessly. We don't pay attention to what we are putting in our mouths. How many of you have eaten a whole bag of chips without even realizing it. On the other hand, eating mindfully enhances the experience of eating and keeps us aware of how much we take in. According to a 2006 American Time Use Survey (ATUS) and Module data Americans age 15 and older spent 67 minutes on an average day in "primary" eating and drinking of beverages. This means that when eating they only eat. Americans spent an average of 16 minutes eating as a secondary activity, such as while working, watching television, or playing sports. It is rare that we simply eat when we eat. When we eat and do other things, the digestive process may be 30 to 40 percent less effective. We also have trouble accurately assessing hunger and fullness. If we are multi-tasking during eating, the brain may not receive critical signals that regulate food intake so it fails to register that we are eating. This causes our brain to continue to send out additional signals of hunger, increasing the risk of overeating.

We need to learn to eat slowly and savor what we eat. Make it an experience, not something you have to get through so you can move on to the next thing that must be done. Slow down and enjoy the moment. Take a short break between bites. Really become aware of the flavors and texture.

Activity:

Pick out a piece of your favorite chocolate. Before placing it in your mouth, smell the chocolate. What do you smell? How does it feel in your hand? Now take a small bite. Hold it on your tongue. What do you taste? Is it really sweet? Can you taste the richness of the chocolate? How does it feel on your tongue? Now chew it slowly. Swallow it. How does it feel going down your throat? How does your mouth feel now that the chocolate is gone? Take another bite and do the same things again. Close your eyes while eating it. What comes to mind when you are eating the chocolate? What emotions do you feel? When you are finished eating the chocolate ask yourself if that one piece was enough or do you want more? When I have done this exercise with people the most common response is that they don't need another piece. The one chocolate was sufficient. Was it sufficient for you?

Hey all you sleep heads, sleep is important! You need to get enough sleep. You should be getting at least eight hours of sleep a night. Lack of sleep causes irritability, forgetfulness, and weight gain. It also can shorten your life. If you have trouble falling asleep you may want to make your bedroom an oasis of relaxation. Don't turn on the television! Use lavender scent on your pillows and sheets. Lavender is great for relaxing. Don't bring any work to bed. Keep distractions at a minimum.

If you still can't sleep, try not to eat too close to going to bed. That means don't eat at least an hour before bedtime. Drink warm milk. Listen to some soft music. Read a book that you can put down. Take Melatonin, a natural sleep aid or drink Chamomile tea.

Activity:

If your mind is keeping you awake, try clearing your mind of unnecessary thoughts by focusing on your breathing. Close your eyes and take a deep breath. Feel your breath coming in through your nose. Is it warm? Is it cool? Feel where your breath goes when you breathe in. Breathe slowly. When you breathe out, how is the temperature of your breath now? Where do you feel your breath? Do you feel it in your lungs or in your stomach? Repeat again, focusing only on your breathing. Keep breathing in and out and just focus on the process of breathing.

Activity:

Another technique, which I used to help me relax because of migraine/tension headaches, is total body relaxation or biofeedback without the wires. Lay down in a quiet place with the lights out. Start with your feet. Tell yourself that your feet are warm, relaxed and comfortable. Repeat this three to five times. Now tell yourself that your ankles are warm, relaxed and comfortable. Then go back and forth from your feet to your ankles. Next add your calves, knees, and thighs. Work your way up your body. Relax your shoulders, neck, and face. Once you practice this technique enough you may find yourself falling asleep before you reach your knees.

One last factor I would like to cover about stress is not prioritizing what you do. How many of us can't say no when asked to do something? How many of us think that everything in our job or in our lives must be done now or must be done at all? Stephen Covey has written about time and its use and devised a four-quadrant chart to help us judge where we spend most of our time. These four quadrants help us to prioritize our activities. These four quadrants are: *Important & Urgent Activities, Important but Not Urgent Activities, Not Important but Urgent, Not Important and Not Urgent.* When you can learn to prioritize your day, this is called "Working in the Zone." In other words, prioritizing means looking at what causes you the most stress and keeps you from you work. To be in this zone is to be free of stress and worry. It means having abundant energy to do what you do best.

The first and highest level of "Working in the Zone," is *Important & Urgent Activities.* These include responding to a crisis, pressing problem, or tight deadline. Most of us on the teaching end of corrections education don't have too many crises to attend to or tight deadlines. Sometimes we have to write up an offender as soon as we can but for the most part if there are any pressing problems or deadlines, we have created them ourselves.

The next level down is *Important but Not Urgent Activities.* These include preventive maintenance, relationship building, creative thinking, planning and recreation. This level is the key to effective management and efficiency. This is where I like to be. I like to be thinking up new ideas for the classroom. You don't have to really be doing anything to be creative. For me it is just sitting in a quiet area, freeing my mind from work and simply letting my mind do its thing. This level is also where people do the schmoozing. Talk to your co-workers; find out what is going on. Some educators make a nice space in their work area for lunch to do their relationship building. It is a nice time to get together, break bread, and talk about what is going on in your lives. This is basically the equivalent to the old "water cooler" scenario in corporations. This level is also my favorite because I can go walking or do some form of exercise. It is an important activity for me so I can get refreshed and energize myself. When you have some down time get a little bit of exercise, go for a drive, run an errand, pick up something to eat, go shopping. Reward yourself - you deserve it.

The third level is *Not Important but Urgent Activities*. These are phone calls, mail, email, meetings and other pressing matters. These tasks are often only urgent because someone else thinks they are! Identify "busy behaviors" or people that drain your time and energy but aren't really important. I have to admit - I love looking to see if I have email. I have several email accounts. I have one for the military, one for work, one for home, and one because I didn't want to cancel it and have to notify everyone of another new email address. I like to get my email taken care of twice a day. I do it as soon as I get to work and once before I eat lunch. I try to answer my email immediately if it needs my attention. I try not to send too many emails that are just about small talk. I want email that is only about business sent to my work email, nothing more. When you start sending and receiving personal emails, then you start receiving all those crazy attachments that take forever to open up. Keep it simple. Personal emails at home, work emails for work.

The final and lowest level is *Not Important & Not Urgent Activities*. These include some mail, trivia, time wasters and pleasant harmless activities. If you spend all your time here, you are totally ineffective. I never go to this level. I like to stay right in the second level. I feel the most productive and comfortable there. I don't like time wasters because I have plenty of other things I can be doing that are worth my time. Sometimes when people are at a loss for what to do, this is where they spend their time. Some time wasters are the telephone and Internet. It's easy to spend a lot of unnecessary time on the telephone or Internet. Time is wasted when you lack a useful purpose for your activities, and when you are easily distracted. Some people justify to themselves that they are working hard when in fact what they are doing may serve no useful purpose. Procrastination is another time waster. Putting things off wastes your time and your physical and mental energy. When you procrastinate, time is wasted because you are not doing anything but thinking and worrying about the things you need to do. Then when you don't get anything done you are mad at yourself. It is a vicious cycle. Lack of organization and tidiness is another time waster. One of the biggest energy wasters is clutter. Clutter not only hinders your effectiveness, but it wastes time as you try to locate things. If you aren't organized you will tend to look through the same mess you looked through the last time. If you can't find something quickly you are not making the most of your time.

Remember don't try to change every problem area in your life all at once. Start with one or two items, and expand as you get things under control.

Activity:

Watch for situations where you feel some degree of stress. Make a note of the situation and what about the situation caused you to feel the stress. Think about how you feel and why you feel the way you do.

Activity:

What level of Working in the Zone do you find yourself in the most? Look at your day and how you use it. Are there time wasters in your schedule? How can you plan your day more effectively to get more things done? What can you eliminate from your day that keeps you from being effective?

Activity: (Think about the following questions.)
1. Do you often feel overstressed?
2. If yes, on average how many days per week?
3. Does stress sometimes interfere with your health, personal happiness, or ability to be productive at work?
4. Is your job often stressful?
5. If yes, in what way?
6. What is causing the main stress in your life?

7. Rank the stress you experience in a typical day on a scale of 1–5; 5 being extremely stressed and 1 being not stressed.
8. Do you get 7 to 8 hours of sleep on a regular basis?
9. Would you consider the sleep you get quality sleep?
10. Are you sometimes unable to relax when you want to?
11. What are some ways that you relax/de-stress?
12. Have you ever tried exercise as a de-stressor?
13. If yes, what did you do and was it effective?
14. List some factors that stimulate stress for you.
15. When you are stressed what do you typically do?
16. If I woke up tomorrow and that stress had vanished, how would know? How would I behave? How would other people know I was different?
17. What are some specific goals that you have related to stress management?

Handle every stressful situation like a dog. If you can't eat it or play with it, just pee on it and walk away. ~ Author Unknown

*Reread the checklist at the beginning of the chapter. Have your thoughts changed?

NEW TEACHER

What happened?
The teacher was eventually terminated.

What could the teacher have done differently?
1. *First of all, no matter what condition his breath was in, you don't bring in toothpaste or anything for an inmate.*
2. *If the offender could not afford toothpaste, the teacher could have referred him to the chaplain. There were other options for the teacher and the offender.*
3. *When the offender asked for more items, the teacher should have stopped right there and reported that she had brought in toothpaste. Now she was bringing in more things. She felt she was in over her head. By nipping it at the bud she would have saved her job.*

Chapter 7

CONFLICT MANAGEMENT

FLOWER DELIVERY

The teacher had been working in a correctional facility for the last three months. One of the offender janitors is assigned to clean her room. The teacher has begun to rely on the janitor to keep her room clean and she has received several compliments on the high level of sanitation her room. The offender has been discussing his personal situation with the teacher. These discussions have included the problems the offender has been having with his girlfriend, that is, that she has been unfaithful to him. The inmate has been calling the teacher by her first name, without her objection.

The other day, the inmate brought her a sandwich from the dining room since she had missed lunch. Although she did not eat the sandwich, she failed to report the situation to her supervisor. Today, the offender left a birthday card on the desk for her. The teacher chose to ignore the card and said nothing about it. When she got home that evening, flowers had been delivered to her home without a card.

What happened and what would you do? (See end of chapter.)

CONFLICT MANAGEMENT

Before you read this section think about the following statements.
Mark each statement:

$\underline{A}$ for agree
$\underline{D}$ for disagree
$\underline{?}$ if you are undecided

1. I avoid the correctional officers.	
2. I feel tension when a correctional officer comes in the classroom.	
3. I complain about everything.	
4. I take things personally.	
5. I avoid all conflict.	
6. I am confrontational.	
7. I am always right.	
8. I look for problems.	
9. I always have to have the last word.	
10. If there is a problem, I go directly to my supervisor instead of working out my problem at a lower level first.	
11. I have trouble communicating how I feel and what I want.	
12. I don't ask questions first I just come out fighting.	
13. I believe I have the power to make the most out of negative situations.	
14. I don't negatively prejudge others.	
15. I am over accommodating to everyone.	

16. I believe I know more than others who may not have the same education I do.	
17. The correctional staff and education staff don't have the same goals.	
18. Interpersonal conflict has no place in the workplace.	
19. I openly challenge others.	
20. I have trouble dealing with others.	
21. People should not talk behind someone's back. Problems should be confronted openly.	
22. Gossip has no place in the workplace.	
23. Cliques have no place in the workplace.	
24. I want things to go my way.	
25. I acknowledge others viewpoints.	
26. I rather work alone than as a team.	
27. Sometimes in order to settle a conflict, we may have to "agree to disagree."	

When good people have a falling out, only one of them may be at fault at first; but if the strife continues long, usually both become guilty.
~ Thomas Fuller

According to Cesar Millan, the Dog Whisperer, "There's a remarkable lack of conflict in dog packs. That's because members resolve the situation when disagreements arise, then move on. Holding onto negative feelings tends to make them multiply and prevent us from moving forward." In disagreements dealing only with the current situation, don't bring up the past.

We have several things we have to deal with in a corrections setting. We have personalities and we have cultures. Working with the conflicting cultures that we have in a corrections setting creates tension, misunderstandings, misconceptions, role confusion, disrespectful interactions and poor communication.

Let's look at the two predominant cultures:

Education	Corrections
Decentralized control	Centralized control
Focused on good of all	Focused on individual
Priority is teaching and learning	Priority is safety and security
Few policies	Policy driven
Academic freedom related to decisions	No freedom related to decisions
Faculty driven activities	Institutionally driven activities

We as educators have a huge balancing act straddling the line between education and corrections. Sometimes we stay more in one culture than the other. When we stay in our education culture, we are sometimes looked at negatively by the corrections staff because we "coddle" our students and bend the rules. In the education culture we are not trying to break the rules, just trying to follow them by asking questions, listening, and coming with the belief that we are doing our best. Correctional educators occupy a difficult dual role. In their relationships with offender students, "they are central figures of authority and control." But when dealing with corrections staff, "they are oftentimes powerless." Few professions in society require a person to constantly engage others from both ends of the authority-compliance spectrum. Sometimes this culture-straddling can cause conflict within the education department and corrections.

If we as educators can learn how to minimize the negative aspects of conflict or how to effectively manage our workplace, our stress can be reduced. The power lies within all of us to create a positive work environment.

By managing conflicts we can:
1. Improve staff communication and conflict resolution skills
2. Improve staff teamwork
3. Improve cooperation
4. Improve morale
5. Reduce conflict among staff

By not managing conflicts:
1. We can destroy morale
2. Impede teamwork
3. Decrease our effectiveness as a department
4. Hurt our relationships

Remember that everyone you meet is afraid of something, loves something, and has lost something. ~ H. Jackson Brown, Jr.

Our attitudes can affect the outcome of conflicts. We have to remember that other people's actions, no matter how painful to us, are simply attempts to meet their needs; so are our own actions. People prefer to meet their needs in ways that don't harm others when they are given options that they believe will meet their own needs. We use this approach when we confront our students' behavior. If a student is misbehaving we give them two options. The first option is to continue doing what they are doing and get written up. The second option is to cease what they are doing and nothing negative will happen. Then ask the student what option he or she is going to choose. Remember, it isn't our needs that are in conflict with each other; it is only the strategies we each employ that come into conflict. When we try to impose our needs on someone we are using the negative strategy of imposing or forcing. We need to employ the strategy of give and take. Another negative strategy is giving up on the other person as soon as conflict exists or seems to be brewing. It is only when we treat others with respect, consideration, and empathy that we can affect the outcome of conflicts.

It is very common to have conflicts at work. We are separated by gender, race, beliefs, and other factors such as tenure or seniority. We also see things differently, want different things, have different personalities, have different goals, and different approaches to the way we do things. We can't afford to focus on only the negatives; we have to focus on what we have in common and our strengths.

Understand the differences; act on the commonalities.
~ Andrew Masondo, African National Conference

We need to work together to solve problems and achieve the same goal of educating our student without conflict. In order to work together we must be honest, respectful, and caring so we can garner trust.

Many times we go about our business at work seeing the pink elephant in the room but just tiptoeing around it. When we have problems with others we may ignore it, talk about it with others at work or at home, but rarely confront it. We end up gossiping, complaining, or just stewing. This can go on for days, weeks, months, or even years until it is too huge to manage and then we have to call in a mediator. If we can confront the conflict early on, get it out in the open, and deal with it, it won't grow into such a huge uncontrollable animal. The other common problem is to hold onto negative feelings even when we supposedly have addressed the conflict. We let those feelings fester and grow until we become unhappy and disgruntled. As a result, we make mountains out of molehills. We let little annoyances get to us rather than just letting them go. We need to ask ourselves, is this little annoyance really little? If it is, why are we letting it bother us like a thorn in a fingernail? Is it something we need to confront with the other person, or is it something we need to confront with ourselves? Sometimes the little things annoy us because it is our problem and no one else's.

Before you criticize someone, you should walk a mile in their shoes. That way, when you criticize them, you're a mile away and you have their shoes.   ~ Unknown

Believe it or not, but we all have some common interests in the workplace. We want to:
1. Have a clear purpose
2. See the results of our work
3. Feel in control
4. Feel competent
5. Be accountable and responsible
6. Be challenged, not bored
7. Be proud of our work
8. Satisfy our customers
9. Communicate and work as a team
10. Be able to grow and learn
11. Be recognized and respected
12. Help others

**(From Search for Common Ground)

Not only can managing conflict at work improve our departments. It can also spill over into our lives outside of prison. We can use the same skills we practice at work to benefit our interactions with our friends and loved ones. Just as our responses to conflict are learned from life experiences, we can also unlearn old responses and create new responses to conflict in the same fashion. To quote Abraham Maslow, "If the only tool you have is a hammer, you tend to see all problems as nails." Therefore, the more ways we have of managing conflict, the more productive we will be.

Conflict provides us an opportunity to do the right thing; choose the right response for the conflict. Most of us fall back on a familiar and comfortable style that we use in conflict situations, but we are all capable of choosing a different style when the need arises.

There are five main types of conflict management styles: Cooperative problem-solving, competing, avoiding, accommodating and compromising.

Cooperative Problem Solving

Cooperative problem solving is the win-win style. People work together to problem-solve. Everyone meets their needs and relationships are maintained.

Characteristics of the cooperative style: (Search for Common Ground)

- The parties see themselves as joint problem-solvers
- Bargaining is based on interests
- Parties make a joint effort to determine facts
- Joint search for underlying interests
- Face-to-face discussions encouraged among all parties
- Workable options are sought
- Yields resolution by integrating interests
- Field of options is broadened
- Characterized by respect and application of reason
- Issues can be identified before positions crystallize
- Authority for decision rests with the parties
- Outcome must be satisfactory to all parties
- Promotes trust and positive relationships

Competing

Just as in any competition, each player wants to win; their interests come first. The competitive style usually only has one winner. This is an assertive and usually uncooperative style.

Compromising

When people compromise they end up satisfying some of their interests because something is better than nothing. Basically you get something and I get something but it isn't necessarily what you really wanted. I do this all the time with my husband. He will ask me what I want to watch on television. There may be several programs I am interested in. I may prefer to watch one over the others but I know that out of those, there is at least one that he wants to watch. So I tell him I want to watch the one I know he will like. It may not be my first choice but I am not unhappy with it and he is happy as well.

Avoiding

When people choose the avoiding style they don't want conflict. They would rather just have someone else decide the outcome. This style is unassertive and uncooperative because the individual doesn't want to participate. This is the style I used to use with my sister. When she would become confrontational, I would simply steer clear of her rather than confronting her. A confrontation would be detrimental to me emotionally and something I couldn't handle. Now I confront her behavior and not her. The scenario continues to be stressful for me, but this strategy works so much better than avoidance.

Accommodating

An accommodator puts their interests last and lets others have what they want. This style is unassertive and cooperative. I think mothers are a good example of this. My mother always put her wants and needs last so we could have what we needed. If we needed money for school clothes, then she would go without things. Many of us are accommodating at work as well because we don't want to stir the pot. We want peace and harmony over conflict.

When we do choose an appropriate style of managing conflict, we also need to be aware of how we communicate. Do we debate or do we engage in dialogue?

The following list is adapted from the writings of Mark Gerzon. He lists the characteristics of debate and dialogue:

Debate
- Assume that there is a right answer and that you have it
- Combative: participants attempt to prove the other side wrong
- It is all about winning
- We listen to find flaws and make counter arguments
- We defend our assumptions as truth
- We tend to critique the other side's position
- We defend our own views against those of others
- We search for flaws and weaknesses in other positions
- We seek a conclusion or vote that ratifies your position

Dialogue

- Many people have pieces of the answer and that together they craft a new solution
- Collaborative: participants work together toward common understanding
- Listening to understand, find meaning and agreement
- Revealing assumptions for reevaluation
- Re-examining all positions
- Admitting that others' thinking can improve one's own
- Searching for strengths and value in others' positions
- Discovering new options, not seeking closure

Both debate and dialogue have their place, but dialogue is what we want to achieve when we are dealing with people, their feelings, and their needs.

How can we improve our behavioral awareness and reduce conflict? First we need to improve our own self-awareness of our core behavior. If you can be more aware of your own behavior, you can become more effective at understanding other people and thereby reducing interpersonal conflict and stress. Help your co-workers become self-aware of their own behavior styles. Ask your supervisor to provide training in personality types and conflict management styles. Through training your co-workers can all be more aware of each other's behavior styles. When we are aware of our own style and the style of others we can learn strengths and weaknesses. We can learn what sets others off and how they would like to be treated.

The best person to start this is you! All it takes is one person's efforts to bring awareness to themselves and their co-workers to make a difference.

I would like to leave you with the following I found from Don Miguel Ruiz, The Four Agreements. It is simple, to the point, and summarizes this chapter:

1. Be impeccable with your words: Speak with integrity. Say only what you mean. Avoid speaking against yourself or gossiping about others. Use the power of your words in the direction of truth and love.

2. Don't take anything personally: Nothing others do is because of you. What others say and do is a projection of their own reality, their own dream. When you are immune to the opinions and actions of others, you won't be the victim of needless suffering.
3. Don't make assumptions: Find the courage to ask questions and to express what you really want. Communicate with others as clearly as you can to avoid misunderstandings, sadness, and drama. With just this one agreement, you can completely transform your life.
4. Always do your best: Your best is going to change from moment to moment; it will be different when you are healthy as opposed to sick. Under any circumstance, simply do you best, and you will avoid self-judgment, self-abuse, and regret.

Activity:

If you are having problems with managing conflict, the following are questions to think about when you are considering choosing a style to manage conflict. While you are thinking about the questions, jot down a few notes.

- Do I care about the outcome? How important is it?
- Is this an ongoing relationship at work or is it a short term one?
- How important is keeping peace and harmony?
- Have I possibly caused the problem?
- Do I have an obligation to manage this problem?
- What are the time constraints?
- What is my intent?
- Do I want to expend the necessary time and energy?
- Will the conflict get worse if I draw attention to it?
- What are the pros and cons?

Activity:

Write down a statement of the problem. Now write down the situation, who is involved? Next consider the other person's perspective. How do you think they perceive the problem? Why do you think this problem concerns them? How do you perceive the problem? Why does the problem concern you?

Activity:

Think of a positive memory of a conflict that was resolved. Write down the reasons that the experience was a good one. What worked? What didn't?

Activity:

Think about the appropriate and inappropriate ways that you meet or have met the following needs: Power, belonging, freedom, fun, and security. What did you do? How was it appropriate? How was it inappropriate?

Go back and reread the checklist at the beginning of the chapter. Have your thoughts changed?

FLOWER DELIVERY

What actually happened?

The teacher in this situation finally reported the flower delivery, which resulted in her having to tell about the other incidents. She didn't lose her job but she did have to undergo retraining.

The teacher should have:

1. *Told the offender that she will not accept the sandwich and reported the sandwich incident. Even receiving an apple should be reported.*

2. *Told the offender to never offer her anything again because it will be reported.*

3. *Told the offender not to call her by her first name and only use her last name.*

4. *Mentioned to her supervisor about receiving the birthday card.*

Chapter 8

TEACHING IDEAS

I WANT YOUR BABY

The teacher smuggled mail in and out of the prison for an offender circumventing the prison's mail-monitoring system. She also let him see an internal staff memo on her education department computer at the prison regarding a confrontation between gang members of different organizations. In addition, she wrote over 35 letters discussing in graphic detail various past sexual acts, the lovers' plans for her to become pregnant and their plans to marry after his release. The teacher had sex with the offender in the education department bathroom on 10 Saturdays.

(See the end of the chapter for the outcome of the teacher's actions.)

TEACHING IDEAS

Before you read this section think about the following statements.
Mark each statement:

$\underline{A}$ for agree
$\underline{D}$ for disagree
$\underline{?}$ if you are undecided

1. I feel comfortable doing what I always have been doing.	
2. I don't believe in creating new lessons because it's easier to reuse older ones.	
3. I don't reflect on what I do in the classroom.	
4. I take advantage of grants.	
5. I am always generating ideas for change in my classroom.	
6. I find renewal after teaching the same course many times.	
7. My teaching never changes based on the make-up of my class.	
8. I seek out resources that help me introduce new ways of teaching in my class.	
9. I keep a folder or file with just ideas for teaching.	
10. I take course evaluations seriously.	
11. I think about how I can manage to make teaching seem fresh and exciting to me every year.	
12. For me, every class is different because they all have different abilities, interests, and passions.	
13. I keep changing so I can keep not only myself engaged but also my students.	
14. I introduce new things in the classroom rather than new ways of teaching.	
15. I've done this before, I am the teacher, and I have been in this game for a long time.	

16. I think about what works and what doesn't.	
17. I want to change but don't know where to start.	
18. I look at my class from my student's point of view.	
19. I am willing to suck it up and try new things regardless if they end up working or not.	
20. I can see an opportunity or make a connection about something that can turn into a great teaching idea.	
21. I see teaching possibilities and take advantage of them.	

If you do the same things you always do, you'll always get the same results. ~ Unknown

Most correctional educators did not know they would end up teaching in prison. Teaching programs don't tell you that you can teach in a prison setting. They only talk about teaching in elementary school, high school, and college settings. Unless you specifically focused on an adult education degree, college programs do not prepare you adequately to teach adults, much less in a prison. Teacher prep programs prepare the teacher to be the one in control of learning, allowing no autonomy for the students. It is important that adult learners and teachers work together actively, and that students be equal partners in their own education. Learners have a tremendous amount of life experiences. They need to connect the learning to their knowledge base. They must recognize the value of the learning. They need it to be relevant and to see the value of lifelong learning in their own lives. For many new correctional educators, this creates a conflict from the start. You have to have the self-confidence to allow your students to set their own personal goals and objectives and be part of the learning process.

Results! Why, I've gotten a lot of results. I know several thousand things that won't work. ~ Thomas Edison

Teaching Ideas You Can Try Right Now:
   Start a book club in the classroom: Order enough copies of books for small groups. You can go online to Barnes and Noble or Amazon and get book club study guides for most books. Or just Google the study guide for the book you are interested in.
   Start a classroom or education newsletter for the offender students: Decide on what you want for the newsletter and get input from your students. This is a great way to get your students to write because they will have a reason to write and that is to get published. You can layout the newsletter using Word. Decide if you want it done monthly or weekly.
   Have students write embassies for information about a country they are interested in: Some students are sent books, maps, and fact sheets on the country of interest. Have the students

100

write a report on the country.

Have students design their own country: Have the class come up with a map, laws, customs, currency, a flag, and so on. Students can then present their country to the rest of the class. They can work in groups or as individuals.

Check out Reading Is Fundamental online: It is an organization that provides grants for free books to children. All you have to do is fill out a simple grant application online and wait to see if you are approved. I had to wait one year but I ended up receiving an 18,000-dollar grant. You have to get 25% matching funds but we ended up with 7,000 books to give out to offender children during two book fairs we sponsored. The men were able to connect with their children through reading books. They chose the books with their children and then read them together.

English doesn't have to be boring: Have students work in groups to make a noun and verb collage. Students cut up pictures and words from old magazines and glue them on poster board to make collages. Let them use colored pencils or markers to add some personal touches to their poster. Students can then present their collage to the rest of the class.

Students can participate in a stock market game: The (Stock Market Game) SMG is available in all states; just Google "SMG" and you will find all the information you need. The cost per team is around $20. Now in our economy would be a great time to help students understand how to invest and save. This game lasts for a couple of months and they can compete against high schools or other adult teams. You will have to buy and sell fake stocks online for the students but the students pick what you buy and sell for them. They have $100,000 to invest and track. The team with the most money at the end wins. You can also invite guest speakers from investment companies to talk to the students.

Get ESL students to learn the parts of the body in English: This activity can be used as a review of terminology already presented. Have students work in groups. One student lies on a large sheet of paper, while another student or students outline him or her on the paper. Display the words for parts of the body on the board. Students are to label the student outline with the words for the parts of the body. For example: elbow, head, calf, and ankle.

The Mathtastic Egg Hunt: Conduct an Easter egg hunt for math. I get plastic eggs that open up. I place math word problems in each egg and hide the eggs. Students can work in pairs or groups to find the eggs. The group who finds the most eggs and also gets each egg word problem correct is the winner.

Math Circuit Training: Set up a hands-on math problem at several tables in the classroom. Students are given a sheet with table numbers. They must go around to each table and work the problem and write the answer on their paper. The individual, pair, or group who finishes all the problems correctly is the winner.

Vocabulary Puzzles: Take sentences with new vocabulary that you have gone over already. Cut the sentences up and place into an envelope. Make enough envelopes of these same cut up sentences for small groups of 3-5 students. Pass out the envelopes and have the students put the sentences together again. They love the competition to see who can complete this quickly.

Find the Mistakes: Pay attention to the newspaper and magazines when you read them. Look for grammar or spelling mistakes. Bring the article and place on the board. Tell the students how many mistakes they are looking for and see who comes up with the mistake and how to fix it first.

Create Your Own Chapter or Booklet: If you know what you want to teach but can't find exactly what you want in a publication and/or if you don't have the funding to buy it, make it. When creating your own exercises, use the names of students in the dialogue or reading examples. Students love seeing their name in print.

Make Your Own Games: For holidays or for specific lesson plans, make bingo games, word finds, or matching games using what you have gone over in class. For instance, make a concentration matching game using vocabulary for the week or math problems.

Using Authentic Materials: What are authentic materials that our students use a lot in prison? Kites and medical requests are probably the most used. Teach your students the words for asking permission and reasons to see someone in position of authority. Have students practice writing reasons to see the doctor or the counselor. Get your students to come up with different scenarios for their Kites. You can work with them on spelling and vocabulary as well.

In addition: Have students -
· Read want ads
· Write resumes
· Type cover letters
· Write work memos
· Read driver's manuals
· Read truck licensing manuals
· Read instruction manuals for household items or office equipment
· Read children's books
· Read fiction
· Read application forms for credit cards or opening a bank account
· Read receipts
· Fill out loan paperwork to buy a car
· Read probation and house arrest rules
· Read diet/exercise books that students can follow in the prison
· Write letters to friends
· Write letters to request something
· Write out lists to keep track of things
· Read recipes
· Read menus
· Read food labels to discover ingredients for health
· Read for religious purposes
· Look at grocery store layouts to locate desired items in store
· Look at grocery ads to learn about prices
· Analyze coupons to discover prices of items and to comparison shop
· Write in journals to record personal responses and thoughts

- Question informational texts to learn new information
- Read buying guides to inform purchasing decisions
- Read cleanser labels safety reasons

There are thousands of ideas you can come up with to use in your classroom. You can get ideas on the Internet or use your own imagination. One way to give my mind a creative jumpstart is to go to a novelty store. I walk around and look at all the crazy and unusual things in the store and then imagine what I could do with them in the classroom. For instance, you can buy little plastic animals or fake fruit and vegetables to use with English language learners.

Activity:
Visit a novelty store. Find 10 things that you could use in your classroom. Can you incorporate them as part of a lesson? Come up with one page per item of how you can use each item as part of a lesson. Now you will have 10 ideas to use in your classroom.

Activity:
Think about the following questions: Are there certain texts that you do not use at all? Are there types of text that you use all the time? How wide a variety of literacy activities do your students currently engage in inside the classroom? Which literacy activities do you think your students engage in outside of the classroom? Which one of those activities do you think would be important to bring into the classroom? Why? What are some ways you can increase active learning on the part of your students?

Activity:
Think about the following questions and answer them: What do you think most students expect in a literacy classroom in terms of materials and activities? What do students need to understand about an approach to teaching that relies upon authentic materials?

Activity:
Think of activities and materials in which students have expressed an interest. How can they be used in the classroom?

Students learn what they care about from people they care about and who, they know, care about them. ~ *Barbara Harrell Carson*

*Go back and reread the checklist at the beginning of the chapter. Have your thoughts changed?

I WANT YOUR BABY

What happened? *(Sorry folks, I have no idea why she did what she did. I could not find any follow-up stories. This is just an example of one of the worst-case scenarios.)*

1. She eventually became pregnant.

2. Because of the internal staff memo she showed to her offender boyfriend, a gang member was stabbed.

3. The teacher pleaded guilty to misdemeanor sexual abuse of a ward.

I am not having sex with a guy who has to work three hours to buy me a soda. ~ *Female Internal Investigator*

Since I don't know the reasons for her behavior and because I could not find any follow up stories about this incident I can't comment on why she did what she did. According to an internal investigator at a correctional facility, most offenders think the only reason women come to work in prison is to find a husband. I am sure we have all heard something like this before. I don't think I need to say anything more on this subject.

Chapter 9

FRESH PERSPECTIVE

Insights from correctional educator David Fickes

FRESH PERSPECTIVE
by David Fickes

As someone new to the world of correctional education, there are aspects of teaching in a prison environment that surprised and frustrated me. Overall, I found the experience enlightening and rewarding.

As background, I am not trained as a teacher, but I have done a great deal of informal and formal teaching in both school and work situations. I have a bachelor's degree in engineering and a masters degree in business and have worked for over 25 years in a variety of technical, analytical, and management roles in large and small companies. Based on a need for teachers and a curiosity on my part, I took a part time contract position teaching vocational math to inmates in welding and computer certificate courses in a medium security prison.

Prior to teaching in prison, I had a reasonable amount of exposure to prison environments through another correctional educator. I had been inside several prisons including maximum-security environments and had interacted with inmates in several situations. That provided me some insight into how prisons operate and what to expect.

The course I was hired to teach covered everything from basic addition, subtraction, multiplication, and division through algebra and geometry in twenty five three-hour evening classes. The students in the class all have either a high school diploma or a GED. In reality, the vast majority have GEDs acquired in prison and often many years earlier so they have little current math exposure. The course is an introductory college course and is accredited towards an associate arts degree.

My typical class has 15-20 students of varying ages from early 20s to 50s. Many had dropped out of school at relatively young ages and had little to no prior success in school environments. Since math is a topic that frequently presents difficulties for people of all backgrounds, there is a large degree of apprehension among the students and a general concern about their ability to succeed.

In terms of teaching methods, I had a basic list of topics that I had to cover and a class textbook. Otherwise, I had pretty much complete freedom as to how I conducted the class. Since I have the ability to solve problems easily on the fly, I chose to make the class very interactive with lots of examples and board work. The textbook became just a jumping off point. I think the students really appreciate the interaction as opposed to more book-based approaches.

Having taught two vocational math courses now over a six-month time frame, I have found the most surprising aspect is the almost childlike excitement and sense of accomplishment that the students get from mastering new things. In my career, I constantly have to teach myself new things; personally, I don't get that same sense of joy that they demonstrate. I think a lot of that comes from most of the students having poor success in prior schooling. On several occasions, I have had students that openly mention that they want to tell their family about how they passed algebra or some particular topic when they had failed it in high school.

One particular frustration that is the counterpart to the excitement of succeeding is the low expectations about their ability to learn new things. Their prior experiences cause them to doubt their ability to learn something like algebra or geometry. When it is presented to them in simple and concise terms, they find that they can learn many things that they didn't think were possible. I continually tell them that they shortchange themselves by saying that they can't do this or can't learn that. Based on my background, I probably overstate at times how simple it is to learn something like algebra since it seems quite basic to me, but I would far rather they assume they can learn anything and approach life from that perspective. From my work background, I am not used to people assuming they can't learn something.

Another interesting aspect I found is that despite their past educational failures and their doubts in their abilities to learn new topics, they have a definite intellectual curiosity. Due to scheduling issues between the evening mealtime and my class, I often have only a portion of the class present for the first hour of the three-hour class. That makes it difficult to cover new topics during that time without necessitating going over the material again for the missing students. Therefore, I looked for ways to occasionally both provide a slightly lighter, more entertaining look at math while trying to show how math applies to the real world since that was one of the common complaints - how would I ever use this.

One night I decided to go over some principles of physics such as speed of light, speed of sound, acceleration of gravity, time for objects to fall a distance, etc. While they didn't necessarily grasp all the concepts, you could see a definite excitement about applying math to everyday concepts and being able determine things like how many miles in a light year, etc. They had obviously heard of some of the concepts like light years or terminal velocity from popular media, but they were genuinely interested in knowing more.

We had a wide ranging conversation over the hour calculating things like how long it would take to fall 30,000 feet and how fast you would be going and what the effect of terminal velocity was and how long it would take to reach the nearest star at the speed of current space ships, etc. They even asked questions like what would happen to the light from a car's headlights if the car were traveling at the speed of light. One student also used the term "infinitely massive" as a comic catch phrase for the remainder of the course after I mentioned that as an object approaches the speed of light it becomes infinitely massive. The things that came up in those conversations were continually referenced by the students during the remainder of the course. That proved to me that they had gotten something out of it, and there was a definite interest in learning for learning's sake.

Overall, my experiences teaching in a prison environment are positive; I am constantly reminded that in many ways the students are no different than people trying to learn anywhere. Due to their past school experiences and their personality types, they probably act younger than their actual age. On the plus side, there is the more childlike joy that goes along with accomplishment that most of us no longer have. On the negative side, there is some of the "I can't do that" attitude that goes along with that. Truthfully, it doesn't occur to me that much that these are inmates or what they may have done. I think they also truly appreciate it when you really try to help them and put in the effort to make topics interesting; they recognize the difference between someone going through the motions and someone who is really trying.

Chapter 10

SMALL MOMENTS LAST A LIFETIME

SMALL MOMENTS LAST A LIFETIME

Small moments, many times. ~ *Eliezer Sobel*

The moments in our lives that stay with us the longest don't necessarily make the headlines. I am sure that we have all had a lot of small and sweet memories that are strong enough to keep us going. Not all of us get to follow up on our former students and find out how they fared. What we do get to see are every day successes in our classrooms. You have a chance to make a difference in the lives of your students and maybe affect the lives of others outside the classroom. What we are able to do with our talents is what keeps us coming back for more. We may not be the runners in the race but we are definitely the cheerleaders. We are the ones standing near the finish line, applauding for the runners who are the slowest, cheering them on. We are the ones telling them that they've done an awesome job and to keep going.

We also inspire our students to go beyond what they are capable of. When I was preparing for my Black Belt test, I practiced breaking boards and cement blocks. My karate Sensei (teacher) would tell me to look beyond what was there and go past the board and block. Aim past what you see. This is our job as well. The things we do in class get our students to look past their limitations and look above and beyond to what can be possible.

One great way to record these special moments and to also reflect on our own teaching is by writing down what we do. Keep a personal journal or publish an article in the *Journal of Correctional Education* or some other literary publication. When you write and publish, you are not only helping yourself but you are reaching out to other educators and sharing what works. You are also inspiring others to try new things. All of you do great things in your classrooms. Don't keep them in the dark. Bring what you do out into the light and let others know about it. The following have been special moments in my teaching:

Multi-cultural Book Club: Students became risk takers. They were more willing to say what was on their mind about what they had read. The students reflected more on the readings and themselves as well as applied themes and storylines to their own experiences. Students

112

who had not read complete books before wanted to read more.

Fathering Program - Children's Book Making: Students not only learned how to write for real authentic reasons, but they also learned computer skills, desktop publishing, and book making. The project gave the men a sense of pride. They learned to connect with their families in a positive and creative way. In turn, the family interacted with the incarcerated member in ways they never thought possible. The project allowed children and family to see the offender in a positive light and reinforced the hope that something good is happening during his incarceration.

Reading Is Fundamental: Offender comments about the program - "I think that the Reading Is Fundamental program is a great program that gives us a chance to bond with our kids in a way that we could not do while incarcerated. I learned more about my daughter by seeing what types of books she picked out to read." "Please keep this program because even if people are in prison they have such a nice opportunity to take advantage of the growth and development of their children by contributing and remaining a part of their lives." "When my children got their books they told me they loved me and thanks dad. They also gave me a kiss over the phone." "My wife was happy that I was able to send the children books from their Daddy." "After receiving the books, my son tried to send me a Thank You cookie!" "I think it is a good way to show your children you care and that reading is a good way to expand your horizons." "I hope that each book opens up the hearts of children and will teach them to love and respect reading." "Thank you for letting me connect with my kids. Even if I can't be with them, when they read that book they think of me."

Spoken Word Poetry: An inmate stands, and uses his two minutes at the mic, to dedicate a poem to a group member that was presently in "the hole" (segregation). After the reading, a friend of mine (Reggie Harris), a visiting poet, asked if any of the members knew where he could find poems of the guy the piece had been dedicated to? From around the circle, men immediately began pulling poems from breast pockets their absent friend had written. "This is why I come into these places," my friend shared, "Where else do you find guys carrying the poems of their friends around with them?"

Theater of the Oppressed: Through games and exercises, the participants learned how to use their bodies and voices expressively. They learned improvisation and dramatic storytelling. They learned how to build pictures, compositions that communicated relationships and how to interpret those pictures. The participants discovered that art is a two-way street - the audience's experience and opinions mattering as much as the artist's.

By the end of the workshops, many of the men had become skilled improvisers, able to tell complex stories and convey character emotions in ways that were clear and engaging. Other expressive skills were also clearly displayed. One moment that particularly struck me was an exercise in composition. The men were asked to name a theme. They chose anger. They were then asked to imagine a moment in their lives where anger was central and to create a static image of that moment using their own bodies. These images were looked at and interpreted very frankly by the others. Then they were asked to arrange the images together in a way that made sense to them. The resulting arrangement told a story of the progression of anger from hurt through a repressed desire for reprisal and acting out of that desire, to incarceration and regret. It was a very powerful image to all the participants and to me.

Oh Romeo, Romeo, Where Art Thou: The students performed the play, Romeo and Juliet. They made the costumes and designed the set. They also published the playbill and came up with the lighting scheme. The men performed for the other classes and the prison staff.

The Taming of the Ghetto Wife: Students rewrote the Taming of the Shrew and made it more up to date. The play took place in a modern-day ghetto complete with guns and drugs. It was a great success and was performed in front of audiences.

It's Never Too Late: Students wrote and published a book about what they did to get into prison and what prison life was like, to deter At-Risk youth from ending up like them. Over 10,000 copies of the book were published. High schools throughout the United States asked for copies as well as National Night Out organizations. In addition, we received letters from parents who were at the end of their rope with their child who said the book really made a difference in their lives.

Christmas Cards: Students made Christmas cards for a senior citizens' home. They also made decorations for the doors of each

114

resident.

Money for Ghana: Students donated money for a school in Ghana. The money bought new uniforms for the children who didn't have any, band equipment, shoes, and school supplies. The teacher in Ghana sent photos of the students receiving their new items to share with the students.

If you are not prepared to be wrong you will never come up with anything original. ~ Sir Ken Robinson

Chapter 11

FINAL COMMENTS

I have tremendous admiration and respect for all correctional educators because I know you are making a difference, whether you think so or not. Your efforts do change lives. I admire you for managing the classroom and the students while putting security first. Bravo! You all are doing such wonderful jobs and you are such inspirations to your students. You have to continue to believe in what you do. I know your job is hard and tiresome. I know sometimes you feel like quitting and finding something else to do. Don't quit. If you don't do this, who will? Who will have the love, compassion, and fortitude to do what you do best?

I have not been immune to feeling burned out and underappreciated. Sometimes I feel like I have given my heart and soul to correctional education and feel completely drained. When I start feeling this way I try to remember the good things that have happened. I try to have faith that if I can get through this one day I am not feeling good about, then tomorrow I will have even more opportunity to do what I do best and enjoy doing it.

My father used to say, "Noli nothis permittere te terere - *Don't let the bastards get you down*." Seriously, he would quote this in Latin. I tried not to disappoint him. There are several things that keep me from getting down and sustain me outside of my own inner strength. That outer strength comes from my belief in God, support from my husband, and the unconditional love of my dog.

I say a prayer every morning to make me an instrument of the Lord's peace and to help me make a difference in the lives of my students. I also pray for the strength and energy to get me through the day.

If you are going through hell, keep going. ~ Winston Churchill

I get my inner strength from taking care of myself mentally and physically. I work out six days a week. I make my workout a priority because it is something I need to do for myself. It keeps my stress low and gives me the energy I need to get through the day. Exercise also makes me feel stronger and in control. My diet is also important. I eat to help me do the things I want to do. I keep my calories at a reasonable level and I don't eat a lot of fat and unhealthy carbohydrates. I also try to get plenty of sleep. I don't care what is on television at night, but I am in bed early enough to get eight hours of sleep.

Some days you're the bug, some days you're the windshield.
  ~ Unknown

The Army and my father have also given me strength. When I went to Airborne school and wanted to drop out because I didn't make the 5-mile run, my dad said, "The Army doesn't like quitters." So I finished the 5-mile run the following week. I have learned to never give up, especially when it means something to you and is important in your life. Being an Army Brat has helped. I moved many times and each time had to start over. I never dwelled on the past. I never looked back, just forward. I just left it all behind me and looked at what I could do with myself at the present moment. How could I adapt and fit in? How could I take advantage of what I had right now? This served me well when I was activated two times with the military: once to Japan and once to D.C. I know I wasn't in a war zone like many of our men and women in the military, but nevertheless, I was gone for a year at a time away from my loved ones and things that were familiar to me. I took advantage of anything and everything that I could. I learned from others and made the most of the time I had. You have to do that in life and in your job.

What also keeps me going are my students. I compare my enthusiasm for coming to school to shell-hunting. When I lived in Panama, I would go looking for seashells everyday. I would look forward to finding a huge, perfect shell. Sometimes I would see the top of what looked like a large Queen Conch sticking out of the mud. I would rush over and pull on it but it wasn't always a whole shell. Sometimes it would be just the top. Other times it would be the whole shell but covered with barnacles and algae. I would have to take the shell home and put it in muriatic acid to clean it up and make it look nice again. My students are like the seashells. Everyday I go to school hoping I will find that big, shiny shell of a student. If I don't find the big shiny shell, then I have to clean him up so he can go out successfully into the world. I don't get disappointed because I know that tomorrow is another day to find those big beautiful shells.

When I feel underappreciated I come home and am greeted by my big wheat-colored, tail wagging, smiling dog, Mr. Tibbs. All feelings of not being appreciated are left at the curb once I step inside my home.

Every once in a while I am reminded that my students appreciate me. Like when I receive a note saying, "Thank you so very much for pushing me and believing in me and most of all for taking the time to work with me. You are a teacher I will never forget and for that I thank you." After graduation when one of my students, who was heading toward retirement pay in my class because he couldn't pass the writing test, came up to me, shook my hand and said, "Thank you for pushing me. I couldn't have done it without you." You can't help but remain positive in this unique world of corrections.

Sometimes it is hard to reconcile the nurturing nature of the teaching profession with the corrections environment. I have to hold back some of myself and yes, sometimes develop the reputation as the "mean teacher." That is because I care but I can't let myself fall into the trap of caring too much. I do put up a defense as someone strong and tough who doesn't put up with whining and complaining in the classroom. I don't believe in excuses and expect the best from everyone because I know they all have it in them.

Don't set limits for yourself. As long as you believe you can do it, go for it. I am always the one wanting to try new things with my students but there is always someone on the sidelines questioning whether I should do it. "Isn't it a lot of trouble?" "Do you have the time?" "Do we have the money?" I have had to be a bulldog about what I want to do and just act on it. I don't try to do things that are against security but I want to bring in new and motivating things for the students to do.

When I was stationed in Japan I wanted to climb Mt. Fuji. There is a Japanese saying that only fools climb the mountain more than once. Call me a fool, but I climbed it twice in one week. If you constantly get told that you can't do things, then look at how you can still do it but in a way that doesn't go against the rules and doesn't harm security. I had a warden tell the education department that we couldn't put things up on the walls since they were newly painted. I hung things up on the ceiling with string and paperclips.

My motto has always been: If I want to do it and I believe in it, I will find a way. I believe if you don't show up and play then you won't win a prize. Ninety percent is just showing up.

Finally, enjoy the ride. When my Special Olympic track athletes compete, it is pure joy. When they run or walk down that track, they want to win but they also want to enjoy the moment. Many of them actually slow down and wave at the crowd and erupt in the biggest smiles you have ever seen. Remember, go with the flow, enjoy the trip, and never let the bastards get you down!

Life is too short. Work as if it was your first day, forgive as soon as possible, love without boundaries, laugh without control, and never stop smiling, even if you don't know the reason. ~ Unknown

BIBLIOGRAPHY

Allen, B. & Bosta, D. *Games Criminals Play: How You Can Profit by Knowing Them*. Roseville, CA.: Rae John Publishers, 1981

"Breakdowns, Complacency are Key Problems in 15-Day Arizona Takeover." *Corrections Digest*. 10 Mar. 2004 <http://www.allbusiness.com/public-administration/justice-public-order/1137791-1.html>.

Cabe, D. "Sweat Yourself Smart: Exercise Makes You Sharper, Happier, and Healthier. Get Ready to Transform Your Life!" *MSN*. 2009 <http://health.msn.com/fitness/ articlepage.aspx?cp-documentid=100230702>.

Cheek, F.E. *Stress Management for Correctional Officers and Their Families*. College Park, MD: American Correctional Association, 1984.

Cooperative Problem Solving: A Guide for Turning Conflicts into Agreements. Washington, D.C.: Search for Common Ground, 2003 <http://www.sfcg.org/resources/training/pdf/cpsguide.pdf>.

Cornelius, G.F. *Stressed Out: Strategies For Living and Working with Stress in Corrections*. Lanham, MD: American Correctional Association, 1994.

Covey, S.R., Merrill, R.A., & Merrill, R.R. *First Things First*. New York: Simon & Schuster, 1994

Cox, M.W. & Alm, R. *Myths of Rich and Poor*. New York: Basic Books, 1999.

Duncan, S. *Present Moment Awareness: A Simple, Step-By-Step Guide to Living in the Now*. Novato, CA.: New World Library, 2004

Dunnigan, J. & Macedonia, R. *Getting It Right: American Military Reforms After Vietnam to the Gulf War and Beyond*. New York: William Morrow and Company, Inc, 1993

"Everest College Study Finds Nearly Half of Washingtonians Worried About Losing Their Jobs." *Reuters*. 28 Apr. 2009. <http://www.reuters.com/article/pressRelease/idUS188714+28-Apr-2009+PRN20090428>.

Fagan, P. "Complacency: The Officer's Number 1 Enemy." *Police One*. 3 Sept. 2000. <http://www.policeone.com/training/articles/44415-COMPLACENCY-THE-OFFICERS-NUMBER-1-ENEMY/Police1.com>.

Forgas, J.P., Lahama, S.M. & Vargas, P.T. "Mood Effects On Eyewitness Memory: Affective Influences on Susceptibility to Misinformation." *Journal of Experimental Social Psychology* 3 Mar 2005: 4, 574-588.

Gehring, T. "Correctional Teacher Skills, Characteristics, and Performance Indicators." *Issues in Teacher Education* 1992: 1, 22-42.

Geraci, P.M. "Professional, Personal and Organizational Identity in a Correctional Education Setting: Can We Be Ourselves?" *In the Borderlands: Learning to Teach in Prisons and Alternative Settings*. Ed. Randall Wright. San Bernardino: California State University, 2006. 1-6

Gibson, B. "Can Evaluative Conditioning Change Attitudes Toward Mature Brands? New Evidence From the Implicit Association Test." *Journal of Consumer Research*. 2008: 35, 178-188.

Goord, G.S. "Commissioner: Staff Complacency Contributed to Escape from Elmira Prison." 19 Mar. 2004. New York State Department of Correctional Services, Office of Public Information. New York State: 2004 <http://www.docs.state.ny.us/PressRel/ElmiraEscape1.html>.

Guimarães, L.H. "Physically Active Elderly Women Sleep More and Better Than Sedentary Women." *Sleep Medicine* July 2008: 9(5), 488-493.

Hanh, T. *Peace is Every Step: The Path of Mindfulness in Everyday Life*. New York: Bantam Books, 1992.

Hash, J. & Wilson, M. "Building an Information Technology Security Awareness and Training." *National Institute of Standards and Technology Special Publication.* Oct. 2003: *800-50*, 1-39. <http://csrc.nist.gov/publications/nistpubs/800-50/NIST-SP800-50.pdf>.

Haynes, A.B. "A Surgical Safety Checklist to Reduce Morbidity and Mortality in a Global Population." *The New England Journal of Medicine* 29 Jan. 2009; 360(5): 491-499.

Hollis, J.F. "Weight Loss During the Intensive Intervention Phase of the Weight-Loss Maintenance Trial." *American Journal of Preventative Medicine* Aug. 2008; 35(2): 118-126.

Jackson, S.E., Schuler, R.S., & Schwab, R.L. "Educator Burnout: Sources and Consequences." *Educational Research Quarterly* 1986; 10(3): 14-30.

James, D.J. And Glaze, L.E. "Mental Health Problems of Prison and Jail Inmates." *Federal Bureau of Justice Statistics (BJS) Report.* Sept. 2006. <http://www.ojp.gov/bjs/pub/pdf/mhppji.pdf>.

Kabat-Zinn, J. *Wherever You Go, There You Are: Mindfulness Meditation in Everyday Life*. New York: Hyperion, 1994

Kashtan, M. "Transforming power relations: the invisible revolution." *Encounter: Education for Meaning and Social Justice.* 2002; 15(3): 10. <http://www.cnvc.org/sites/cc.org/files/transform-power-relations.doc>.

Kern, T. *Redefining Airmanship.* New York: McGraw-Hill Professional, 1997. 273.

Knudtson, M.D., Klein, R. and Klein, B.E.K. "Physical Activity and the 15-Year Cumulative Incidence of Age-Related Macular Degeneration: the Beaver Dam Eye Study." *British Journal of Ophthalmology* 31 Oct. 2006; 90: 1461-1463.

Lindsay, S. *Handbook of Applied Dog Behavior and Training, Volume Two: Etiology and Assessment of Behavior Problems.* Iowa: Iowa State University Press, 2001.

Lofshult, D. "Eat Slow and Carry Less Weight." *IDEA Fitness Journal* Feb. 2009; 6(2).

McCampbell, S.W. & Layman, E.P. "Investigating Allegations of Staff Sexual Misconduct With Inmates: Myths and Realities." *Sheriff Magazine* Dec. 2001; 53(6): 20-23.

Merchant, C. "Preventing, Preempting, and Resolving Conflicts in the Workplace." *Head Start Bulletin.* 2000: 68 <http://eclkc.ohs.acf.hhs.gov/hslc/resources/ECLKC_Bookstore/PDFs/0AE4194A07F88FD3DFEAF7D4FBD57273.pdf>.

Millan, C. "What Your Pet Can Teach You." *Parade Magazine.* 1 Jan. 2009. <http://www.parade.com/pets/articles/090111-dog-whisperer.html>.

Ruiz, D.M. *The Four Agreements: A Practical Guide to Personal Freedom.* San Rafael, CA: Allen Publishing, Inc., 1997. Front Flap.

Schlesinger, R. "Better Myself: Motivation of African Americans to Participate in Correctional Education." *Journal of Correctional Education* 2005; 56(3): 228-252.

Shackell, E.M. & Standing, L.G. "Mind Over Matter: Mental Training Increases Physical Strength." *North American Journal of Psychology* 2007; 9(1): 189-200.

Spencer, H.T. & Shuford, J.A. "Experiential Conflict Resolution for Prison Staff." *Corrections Today* 1 Dec. 1999; 61, 1.

"The American Workplace - How Much Time Do Americans Spend At Work?" *Chartbook of International Labor Comparisons: The Americas, Asia/Pacific, Europe* (U.S. Department of Labor, Jan. 2008, 14). <http://digitalcommons.ilr.cornell.edu/cgi/viewcontent.cgi?article=1489&context=key_workplace>.

Thomas, T.F. *Conflict Management and Conflict Resolution in Corrections.* Lanham, MD: American Correctional Association, 1999.

Tolle, E. *The Power of Now: A Guide to Spiritual Enlightenment.* Novato, CA: New World Library; Vancouver, B.C.: Namaste Publishing, 2004.

Topham, J. "Sting!" *Correctional Compass.* Apr. 2000 <http://www.dc.state.fl.us/pub/compass/0003/page03.html>.

Vaananen, A. "Effects Predictability at Work and Risk of Acute Myocardial Infarction: An 18-Year Prospective Study of Industrial Employees." *American Journal of Public Health* 2008; 98(12).

Warburton, D.E., Katzmarzyk P.T., Rhodes, R.E., and Shephard, R.J. "Evidence-Informed Physical Activity Guidelines for Canadian Adults." *Canadian Journal of Public Health* 2007; 98(2): 16-68.

Werfelman, L. "Unsafe Acts." *[Electronic version]. AeroSafety World.* 2007; 52-54. <http://www.flightsafety.org/asw/june07/asw_june07_p50-52.pdf>.

Wheeler, T. "Choosing a Conflict Management Style." *Ohio Commission on Dispute Resolution and Conflict Management.* 1995 <http://disputeresolution.ohio.gov/schools/contentpages/styles.htm>.

Wilson, A. *Ziggy.* 2001 <http://www.ziggyzone.com>.

Teaching on the Inside:
A Survival Handbook for the New Correctional Educator
by Pauline Geraci

$12.95
(Plus $3 shipping and handling)

To place an order, or to request a free catalog of
more resources for correctional education, please contact:

Greystone Educational Materials
P.O. Box 86
Scandia, MN 55073
Phone: 1-800-733-0671
Fax: 1-800-642-2791
greystoneedmat@frontiernet.net

ABOUT THE AUTHOR

Pauline Geraci has been an educator for over 16 years. She has a BA in Elementary Education, an MA in Reading Education, and a certificate in Teaching English to Speakers of Others Languages.

In 1999, and again in 2001, Geraci received the Marvin Sull Award for creative teaching that impacts inmates in the classroom and the community. Geraci has also been nominated twice as Teacher of the Year, at New River Correctional Facility in Florida and at Minnesota Correctional Facility - Stillwater.

Pauline has presented at both international and national corrections conferences, is a grant writer and author of Teaching on the Inside, as well as co-author of two books with her offender students, It's Never Too Late and The Choice is Yours. She has also been published in the anthology, In the Borderlands: Shaping a Professional Teaching Identity in Prisons and Alternative Settings, and the *Journal of Correctional Education*. In addition, she is the producer of the video, The Stillwater Poetry Group.

Ms. Geraci is a member of the Commission of Adult Basic Education, the International Reading Association, the Correctional Education Association, and the Washington Correctional Association.

Pauline is currently an officer in the Army Reserve and has been in the military for over 24 years. She is also a certified personal trainer, kettlebell and boot camp instructor, healthy behaviors coach, Special Olympics track coach and has a black belt in karate.